HIGHEST TRADITIONS

Other works by this author:

Never Trust A Man In Curlers
Looking For
Tale Of The Toy Soldier
Company Stock
Buddies

for Ted.

7/9/2021

HIGHEST TRADITIONS

Memories of War
Tony Lazzarini

Always good to see you.

Best wishes

Tony Lazzarini

VOYAGER PUBLISHING • GREENBRAE, CA.

"We few, we happy few, we band of brothers;
For he today that sheds his blood with me
Shall be my brother . . ."

– Shakespeare, *Henry V*

Dedication

In respectful memory of Staff Sergeant Richard Barton. My own personal hero. My "Uncle Dick."

Foreword

I don't know why it's taken me so long to write this book.

I apologize to other Vietnam veterans for not letting people know of the great deeds done by them. These were young men and women caught in a part of history that evolved from a series of misconceptions and lies. Sixty-one percent of the fatal casualties never reached their 22nd birthday.

Most early Hollywood movies did not portray the true image of the Vietnam veterans.

Local and national news media were quick to report any act of violence involving a Vietnam vet, adding to the fallacy the war had turned us all into walking time bombs that could go off at the slightest provocation. I cannot recall how many times I was told I seemed "so normal" after stating the fact I had fought in Vietnam.

The following incidents are from missions I flew as a helicopter door gunner in Vietnam during my twenty-one months of service. They revolve around the men of "A" Company, 25th Aviation Battalion, 25th Infantry Division. We flew by the call sign, "Little Bear." Our 25 UH-1D helicopter company was composed of two assault platoons and a VIP platoon. This model aircraft was commonly referred to as "Slicks" because they lacked mounted weapons, other than an M-60 machine gun on each side.

Helicopter aircrews in Vietnam suffered many casualties. Of the approximately 12,000 helicopters serving during the extent of this war, 7,013 were UH-1's. Huey only losses were 3,305 helicopters, 1,074 pilots and 1,103 crewmembers. The names of 35 Little Bears are permanently etched on the Vietnam Memorial Wall.

In 1966, A Company became the most decorated air-mobile helicopter group in Vietnam. By the end of the war, the Huey would end up having more combat flight time than any other aircraft in the history of warfare. The Huey was a constant part of the sky as the sun and stars. The popping sound made by the rotor blades announced its arrival and departure. It was a supply ship, a Medevac ship, a transport ship, a weapon to fear and many times heroically denied the Grim Reaper his take.

As you read these stories, please remember that thousands of crewmembers like me were doing the same thing throughout Vietnam before they reached the legal age for drinking or voting in the United States.

The Valorous Unit Citation Award is awarded by direction of the Secretary Of the Army to:
THE 25th AVIATION BATTALION
and attached units:
53rd Aviation Detachment (Provisional), 269th Aviation Battalion
116th Aviation Company, 269th Aviation Battalion
118th Aviation Company, 145th Aviation Battalion
for extraordinary heroism

The 25th Aviation Battalion and assigned and attached units distinguished themselves by extraordinary heroism while engaged in military operations on 19 July 1966 south of the Saigon River in the Ho Bo Woods, Republic of Vietnam.

After two infantry platoons were helilifted into hostile territory, they made contact with well-entrenched Viet Cong units and requested armed aircraft support. Gunship crews of the 25th Aviation Battalion aggressively engaged the hostile forces, flying fearlessly at tree top level through intense ground fire.

Despite the increasing barrage, these gallant men effectively suppressed the enemy and prevented them from inflicting heavy losses on the besieged forces. As the violent firefight continued, transport helicopter crews selflessly braved the hostile fire and landed friendly troops within 150 meters of the line of contact.

Later in the day, 25th Aviation Battalion transport helicopters were requested to extract friendly elements from the battlefield. Because the Infantrymen were still savagely engaged and casualties were scattered throughout the pickup zone, pilots valiantly maneuvered their aircraft from point to point, touching down within two meters of wounded men so that door gunners could quickly lift them inside. Heedless of many hits to the aircraft, the crews repeatedly descended into the ravaged zone and rescued numerous stricken soldiers. The selfless, unremitting combat support rendered by these aviators stands as an admirable example of indomitable fighting spirit and dedication to the free world counterinsurgency mission.

The men of the 25th Aviation Battalion and assigned and attached units displayed extraordinary heroism and devotion to duty which were in keeping with the **highest traditions** of the military service and reflect distinct credit upon themselves and the Armed Forces of the United States.

Table of Contents

Door Gunner

In 1965 I was stationed in Hawaii with the 25th Infantry Division. I was trained as a helicopter mechanic, and A Company, 25th Aviation Battalion had a small fleet of CH-21 "Shawnees." They were usually referred to as "flying bananas" because of their shape. They had rotor blades fore and aft and were normally used for transporting supplies or troops. They were old, noisy, rattled, and powered by an eighteen-cylinder twin bank radial engine. We kept busy after every flight repairing stress cracks in the airframe. They were later replaced by the twin turbine CH-47 Chinooks. The army named all their helicopters after Indian tribes; I never did figure out why.

One day, I had passed by a corporal in my company wearing a patch on both shoulders. I knew one was our division patch because I also wore one but the other, on his right shoulder, known as a combat patch, I did not recognize. Over his left pocket he sported a set of flight wings. I had to ask him what that was all about.

"That's a MAC V patch (Military Assistance Command-Vietnam) and the wings are gunner's wings," he said. "I went through door gunner training here in Hawaii, and later was sent to Vietnam for 90 days TDY (temporary duty)."

The division had a program known as "Shotgun," after the shotgun riders on the stagecoaches of the early west. They trained volunteers to act out this modern day version to protect helicopters in a place called Vietnam. Being 19 years old, it sounded cool to me. I never had to volunteer for the program because the entire 25th Infantry Division went over a few months later. I went through a gunner program because A Company wanted everyone trained who might be flying later.

It was my first ride in a UH-1 Iroquois. Yep, another Indian name but they would become better known as the Huey. A turbine driven, nice riding, high-powered piece of flying hardware. It was a 1300 horsepower roller coaster on wings. (Actually rotor blades, but you get my drift.) None of us knew at the time a whole new way of fighting would be developed around these aircraft.

Our Huey Slicks had two post-mounted M-60 machine guns, one on each side, that could pivot in all directions with built in front and rear stops so an anxious gunner could not accidentally shoot down his own ship. A metal tray at the base of the mount held 300 rounds of ammo and fed the gun through a flexible metal chute. In Vietnam, we eliminated the chute because of problems with ammo binding in it under extreme twisting conditions. If the ammo stopped moving, the machine gun quit firing. We also tossed the 300 round containers. Our machine guns fired 400 rounds a minute. Who the hell ever figured out that combo? In country, we found that by reinforcing a smoke grenade box and securing it to the bottom of the machine gun mount we could link up about 1500 rounds. Much better.

A Huey crew consisted of the AC (aircraft commander), pilot, crew chief and gunner. The AC was usually the ranking, more experienced officer and flew the ship. The co-pilot monitored the vast array of gauges and kept the AC informed of changes. He also took over the flight controls if the AC became disabled. If the co-pilot happened to be a fresh replacement, he bore the listless title of "peter pilot," referring to the fact they "didn't know dick!" (My own interpretation.) The crew chief performed all of the daily maintenance on the ship and acted as the door gunner on the other side of the helicopter. We could load up to seven grunts and all their gear. The chief kept us flying and I kept the guns working. He and I were the only ones assigned to a specific aircraft. It was *ours*!

13

Specialist E-5 Jerry Spurlin, the crew chief, and I flew "Little Bear 626." All ships were known by the last three digits of their tail number and would be spoken individually. Six two six would fly countless missions and log hundreds of hours of combat time before it became a mass of broken aircraft scattered on the Tan Son Nhut runway.

Jerry was a soft-spoken kid of slender build with a dry sense of humor and a ready grin. With his GI glasses, he looked like he would be more at home in a library hovering over books than sighting down the barrel of an M-60 machine gun. He and I were 19 years old, a couple of years younger than the pilots.

Base Camp

After 23 days chugging across the Pacific Ocean in a WW II Liberty Ship, land looked mighty good. The main elements of the 25th Division arrived in Vietnam April 30th, 1966.   Infantry battalions had arrived a few months earlier to secure an area for our base camp. The area we occupied was an old peanut plantation. Cu-Chi (pronounced Coo-Chee) would be our home for the next 12 months. The camp lay outside a zone called the "Iron Triangle." This zone would be our main area of combat operations and reported to contain an estimated 10,000 Viet Cong.

From our debarkation point, we were flown by cargo plane, helicopter and finally arrived by truck. A large piece of dirt-covered property was presented to us as our "home." I doubled up with a buddy and up went the pup tent. There weren't a lot of facilities the first few months. We changed clothes when they were dirty and showered in the rain. Our main duty of the day was filling sandbags to make bunkers.

Vietnam has two climates: "hot and wet" and "hot and dry." Shirtless in the heat, we would fill bags for hours with the powdery dirt of the old plantation. It clung to us like a second skin. Sandbags for bunkers, sandbags for walkways, sandbags for walls around the hooch. Sweat from our foreheads would relentlessly dribble down the front of our faces to sting our eyes. Salt tablets and malaria pills were part of our daily meal.

Later, rumbling C-130 cargo planes would skim the dirt-covered runway and eject ten-man tent kits from their rear cargo doors. For months we slept under GI canvas on folding cots under mosquito netting. We moved on to hooches with thatch-covered roofs and wooden sides. Depleted ammo boxes and vacant rocket pallets made up the walls. Someone scrounged a fuel wing tank from an F-4 jet. We built a platform similar in looks to a wooden oil well derrick and sat the tank on top of it pointing straight up. Cold water came from a hand dug well. That gave us a good supply of water to run a four-showerhead operation. Unfortunately we didn't have showerheads so on/off spigots were used. They shot out a one-inch thick stream of ice-cold liquid. Fourteen months later we devised a way to have hot water. After that, life just kept getting better.

The first EM (enlisted men) mess hall was an open ten-man tent set on soil packed hard from the constant parade of combat boots. It provided park benches with tables and shiny tin café style napkin dispensers that would make you laugh when you noticed puncture holes from previous mortar attacks.

Bathrooms were not elaborate. A small, enclosed wooden structure with accommodations for three or four. Sitting side by side, it was easy to carry on a conversation with your neighbor due to the absence of partitions. The participants sat on a plywood box that sported *actual* toilet seats. Deposits were made into fifty-five gallon steel drums cut in half. These were dragged out each morning, their contents doused in diesel fuel and burned. This highly popular event was cleverly entitled "the shit burning" detail. Each morning, columns of smoke drifted across the base camp like an ominous black fog.

Our entire area of combat operation was fairly flat, covered with trees, jungle, marshes and various shades of green and brown rice paddies that checkered the landscape.

Thirty miles northeast of us stood Nui Ba Den (Black Virgin Mountain). It was the only mountain for hundreds of miles. About 3200 feet high, it just sort of stood there in defiance of all that flatness.

Our aircraft was parked a football field length away from the main company area, each sitting silently in an L-shaped wall of sandbags piled five feet high to protect them against the occasional incoming mortars.

We had to scatter them across the base camp when suspecting a possible attack. Helicopters were a constant source of misery for the enemy. They would go to any means to destroy one. Many nights I guarded 626 alone and gazed at the night sky wondering if I would ever shave with hot water again in front of a mirror. It was the little things I missed.

Equipment

The M-60 machine gun was the life support for all Slicks. How well it operated determined whether or not you would survive a "hot LZ" (landing zone under fire). It was the basic model the infantry units used with a few minor changes. The standard guns fired about 400 rounds a minute. It took a 7.62 mm cartridge, the same size used in the infantry's M-14 rifle. The M-60 was the best twenty-four pounds of weapon in the army. Operators were instructed to shoot in short bursts – maybe 10-20 rounds – to keep the barrel of the weapon from overheating. Overheated barrels could distort and render the machine gun useless. Another problem was a "cook off," a shell exploding in the barrel chamber from the heat caused by the previously fired rounds.

It was all about firepower when we were in a combat situation, so the more rounds we could get off, the safer we could keep our ships and the ground troops while they were boarding or unloading. We were able to slow the firing rate to 300 rounds a minute and fire longer bursts. Another factor was, we were moving through the air so basically our guns became "air-cooled." I often fired bursts of over 100 rounds at a time. The barrels of M-60s were replaceable with the flip of a lever. Gunners carried a spare barrel and an insulated glove to replace a hot barrel if necessary.

We also used a twin grip curved "butterfly trigger" assembly. It relocated the trigger from the middle of the machine gun to the rear, similar to a .50-caliber machine gun. That way we were able to aim and fire with one hand, and feed the ammo with the other. We found that a large C-ration can would clip into the receiver area of the machine gun and the linked ammo flowed right over the top without binding. I got rid of the chute and replaced the tray with a box that held 1500 rounds of tracers.

When non-gunner types questioned me about the unopened C-ration can labeled "Ham with Lima Beans and Water Added," hanging on the side of my machine gun, I told them I was just heating up chow.

We each carried our own M-16 rifles for back up. It was a great weapon if you ever fought a war in a vacuum. It was very susceptible to dirt and dust. Their tendency to jam when hot was later engineered out by the manufacturer.

Personal protection came in two types. For low-risk missions, most of us flew with a standard flak vest. It was lightweight, fit like a standard vest and would probably stop flying metal from grenades or bits of aircraft fragmented by enemy rounds. When we knew we would be flying a C/A (combat assault) and expected heavy fire, we switched to the "chicken board." The board was a chest protector made of hard pressed metal with a porcelain cover. It was wrapped in the always-popular olive drab green colored fabric and secured to your body by Velcro straps. It protected your upper torso and could stop most small arm rounds. It was heavy and awkward. One of the gunners had taken a hit on one. The impact of the round knocked him back, but did not penetrate the board. Pilots wore them constantly because of their exposed position at the controls of the Huey.

The "monkey strap" was a harness kind of affair. It fit over your shoulders and around your waist. It was anchored at the bulkhead behind the gunner and had enough lead (about six feet) to let you maneuver outside the ship without having to undo and reconnect the standard seat belt hookup. It had a huge drawback. In the event you had to exit the ship in *one big hurry*, most guys forgot to unsnap it and it would jerk them back against the helicopter like a giant rubber band. I never wore one.

Since we were flying, most enemy rounds came up from under the seat. I used this area to store extra ammunition for both guns. The heavy containers made a great protective barrier. My minimum supply of ammo for both guns was usually 4000 rounds.

A collection of different colored smoke grenades hung within reach on the vertical post used to mount seats. White was used to mark areas where we encountered enemy action. We could return to the area immediately to search out the sniper or call for help from Huey gun ships or F-4 fighter jets.

We carried whatever else we thought we might need: hand grenades, tear gas grenades and sometimes a small block of C-4 explosives. I liked the C-4 because you could break off a chunk and use it to heat up a can of C-rations. If we did not have anything handy to heat up food, we would drain a little fuel out of the Huey into a small can filled with dirt and use that as our stove. I kept a piece of 4 by 4-inch metal screen on board which I could use as my grill. Needless to say, we only cooked when parked out in the boonies.

Good shot of the C-ration can on the M-60

Building tent kits

Some of the "Little Bear" door gunners

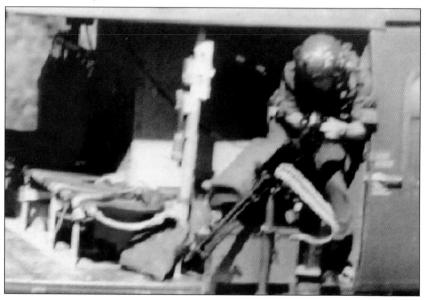

What we look like from the outside

The Gunners

We hung out together, drank together and fought together, sometimes among ourselves. Just about every night, we would end up at the EM club drinking Budweiser. Some of the Asian beer was so bad we used cases of it to build steps or walkways. We actually built the club ourselves. It was an A-frame structure with two large wings on each side.

Occasionally the officers would put on a barbecue out front and we would all hang out together eating steaks and swapping stories. Coming back late after a mission usually meant dinner that night would be pepperoni sticks and peanuts at the club. At the gunners' table next to the jukebox, we would go over the day's events, talk about who was getting short

27

(about to return to the states) or maybe about our exploits on R & R (Rest and Relaxation). We would play songs on the box. The floors were wooden and built above ground. If someone played a song we didn't like, we just stomped our feet. The vibration would cause the needle to skip across the record and it would end abruptly. Nobody dared complain because we were "the gunners."

It was surprising how much alike we were. No one was older than 22. The states were well represented: Alabama, Kentucky, Illinois, California, New York, Texas, New Mexico, Rhode Island. Conversation was a clash of accents. Door gunners were volunteers. That told you something right there. In training, I was told the average life span of a helicopter door gunner in a hot LZ was 20 seconds. Flying in and out of trouble was a huge adrenaline rush. War to us was a go and get in it kind of thing. Nothing got us more jacked up than knowing we would be flying combat assault the next day. "Full suppression" was a term that meant we would be going in and firing our machine guns at anything that held the enemy, looked like it could hold the enemy or looked like something that looked like it could hold the enemy. We all became adrenaline junkies. I felt a little sorry for the pilots. We were in the back having all the fun and they were just driving the bus. We would fly into hot LZs with helicopter gunship escorts discharging rocket after rocket, pounding the earth with black and orange fireballs that saturated the air with the stink of burnt foliage and black powder. It was the combination of flight, noise, and danger but never the possibility of death.

Everyone knows that at twenty you are invincible. Soldiers bleeding, downed Hueys, smoldering ashes whipping around a helicopter caught in the violent turbulence of its rotor blades. Shoot anything that moves. We had the sixth sense that protected only the chosen few. The unlucky could only be remembered for a short while. New people, new ships, new missions, the next mission, that's all there was. Get ready, stay prepared, stay loose, and smoke 'em when you got 'em. You are known for what you do. There is no hiding, lying or cheating. Bullshit carries no weight. Your word, your action, your machine gun is who you are. Period.

The Pilots

I flew with some pretty amazing pilots. Most of them were in their early 20's. The youngest ones were Warrant Officers, usually 19 or 20 years old and fresh out of flight school. They had to be able to stay loose. When the bullets started coming in our direction, I could just pull back on the trigger of my machine gun and feel I was doing something productive. All the pilots could do was hang on to the flight controls in front of a fairly visible cockpit and fly the ship. One thing they had over us in the way of protection was an armor-plated seat. The pilots were protected on three sides and the bottom leaving them exposed only from a head-on position. Removing a pin at the bottom rear of the seat would enable it to tilt back, so an injured flyer could be moved away from the flight controls and attended to. Taking off, the nose of a Huey is in a tilted down attitude in order to develop lift, making the pilots most vulnerable.

Nothing ever got by in Vietnam. If you were good everyone knew it. If you were bad, everyone knew that too. Bad meant you were wound a little too tight to handle the pressure, or you just made really stupid decisions that put the entire crew in danger, and not just once.

The worst for me was a major who flew just enough hours a month (four) to remain eligible for his flight pay. He would pick a milk run "ash and trash" mission. These were mostly flown over very secure areas, or as secure as we could get. Pick somebody up here, drop him off there. The basic taxi driver routine.

The first incident happened while flying into Tan Son Nhut from our base camp. Standard run. Apparently, he never got around to reading the procedures about dropping to a low altitude when crossing the air force base runway outside of Saigon to avoid colliding with some big frigging airplane.

I had just enough time to yell out over my headset, "Aircraft at nine o'clock!" I felt as if my entire body was ready to explode. We dropped like a rock when he forced the ship into a dive. I glanced up to see the landing gear of the transport plane retracting into their compartments as it passed overhead.

Dying in a confusing and unpopular war is bad enough but dying in it by accident would really piss me off!

The second occasion was equally as bad, and only sheer luck kept eleven of us alive that day. When people ask me, "What was the closest to dying you ever came?" this incident always comes to mind.

Setting up blocking forces is a common strategy in warfare. A group of ten helicopters would unload a company of infantry at one end of an area to sweep through, forcing all in their path to go in the opposite direction. By then, we will have picked up another group of men to be the blocking force and catch the exiting enemy. We loaded up our first body of men at our base camp in the morning and dropped them into position. I was flying trail, last ship of the group. We flew back and picked up the second force and waited with these men at a forward artillery base close to the operation. With nine helicopters leading us in, we started our approach onto the base to sit and wait. It was the hot and dry season. The rain-drenched mud from the previous months had now turned to a powdery dust reducing visibility to almost nonexistent when whipped by rotor wash of the helicopter's blades.

We were lagging behind. I'm sure it was because of our pilot's inability to fly in close formation. With dust flying all around and visibility poor, he must have thought it would be safe to put the ship down where he assumed was close to our main group. The skids hit the ground and I was just about to exit the ship when the panicked voice of our flight leader yelled on my headset, "Trail, you're in a mine field!" I pulled back quickly and motioned to the grunts to stay seated. Sure enough, a few feet ahead of us stood the wire perimeter fence separating us from the camp. With fuel cells holding hundreds of gallons of jet fuel in the belly of the helicopter, even a small explosion would have been devastating. Somehow our skids had managed to avoid contact with the buried mines. Picking back up slowly, we made the short hop over the fence to safe ground.

I don't recall that major flying any more missions.

There were some great pilots. The best ones encouraged you to exchange seats with the other pilot and learn to fly the machine. My first experience as a novice aviator was with a 24-year old 1st Lieutenant named John Kulhavi. We were up about 2000 feet so he would have plenty of time to regain control if I became a little overzealous. I don't remember the exact air speed, but I'm sure it was somewhere around 70 knots. The two main controls on a helicopter are the "collective" and the "cyclic." The collective gives you up and down and the cyclic controls lateral direction – left, right, front, rear or a combination.

I was a helicopter mechanic before becoming a gunner and familiar with the flight controls and theory, but this was the first time I had an opportunity to actually fly one of these things. John told me to put my hand on the cyclic and said, "Just think where you want it to go." I had seen a lot of John Wayne pictures when he was playing the part of a fighter pilot. It was in the days when planes had those stick controls that came up between the pilot's legs. All a guy had to do was swing that stick in the direction he wanted to go and that's where you went. I felt pretty good holding the flight controls while John was backing me up on his. I was checking the instrument panel making sure I was at least flying level when John mentioned that the air speed was falling off and I should "drop the nose a little." Well like good old Captain Wayne did in "Flying Leathernecks," I shoved the stick forward. Down – and I mean down – we went. Talk about touchy! A one hundred-mile-an-hour ride in an elevator! Lt. Kulhavi quickly recovered control, then handed the ship back over to me. From then on I was the most "thinking" guy who ever flew a helicopter. He must have had a lot of faith for he continued to let me in the seat whenever there was an opportunity. We would fly numerous missions together including ones into Cambodia in an unmarked Huey and no U.S Army ID on any of the crew. We trusted each other with our lives.

A few months after I left for home, a friend wrote to tell me Kulhavi had been shot down and the crew suffered casualties. Lt. Kulhavi was wounded but would recover. Today he is Brigadier General John G. Kulhavi and, I'm proud to add, still my friend.

I flew with a young 1st Lieutenant named Jack Zelsman on his first combat mission. We would be going into an area known to be hot. Like all good officers, he was doing the pre-flight on our ship just before we went over to the staging area to hook up with the grunts. This was about my 100th mission and I was checking him out as thoroughly as he was checking out the ship.

I think he wanted to impress me with his knowledge of machine guns, because he made a point to ask if both guns were clean and ready to go.

"Yes Sir!" I snapped back. We were both standing directly in front of my gun, which hung on its mount with the barrel facing down in its locked position. He pulled the gun up to a horizontal position, flipped the locking lever for the barrel and pulled it away in his right hand. The gun barrel has a small moving part in it that, when clean, slides back and forth and produces a little "click" as it reaches the end of its travel in both directions. He rotated the barrel top to bottom listening for this telltale sign. These were *my* guns. Anytime a round went through them, they were completely pulled apart and every piece inspected, lubricated, cleaned or replaced. It was almost an insult to me.

Satisfied with the reassuring sounds, the Lt. slid the barrel back into the receiver of my machine gun and swung it down to latch it in place. What he forgot to do was flip the lever to secure the inspected barrel. Halfway through its downward arch, it became airborne and found its way into a muddy puddle left from the previous night's rain. Silence. He looked at me and I looked at him the way a person would do at a small puppy that was just caught dumping on the dining room rug. I could not spank him, because after all, he's just a puppy. "You better get that cleaned up," was his weak attempt at face-saving, and the only words to escape his mouth. I had a feeling it was going to be a very long day. Little did I know at the time, this pilot and I would also become good friends. Could that guy drive a Huey!

Missions

If there was something to do in Vietnam it probably required a Huey. The Bear platoon I was in was involved in combat operations, but also used in the day-to-day operation of our large base camp at Cu-Chi. These were happily known as the ash and trash missions.

We hauled troops, and constantly supplied them in the field with food, blocks of ice, ammo or whatever else they needed. Our flight operations assigned the missions for each ship the previous night. It was a small something to look forward to and gave us time to make any changes to the ship the new mission may require. I would always load up with extra ammo for assaults and good reading material if we were going to be sitting out in the boondocks waiting for someone or something to arrive.

We had great missions such as courier, mail runs, leaflet drops, counter mortar, medevac, and transportation.

Dull as these seemed, they were still in country with a high possibility of getting shot at or even shot down. We took them all seriously, but managed to have a little fun now and then. It always felt good to pick people up and start them on their way back to the states. We tried to do something extra special if it was one of our own guys. Just before departure, we would take a couple of smoke grenades – nice colors like yellow or red – and tape them to the skids on each sides of the ship. Once our passenger was dropped off, we pulled the pins and circled around them. The colors would become a floating streamer, then dissipate in the thin hot air. I wondered if I would ever see that sendoff from the ground.

Occasionally we lucked into picking up a celebrity who came to entertain the troops. One day I had Dale Robertson and a few of his entourage come on board. He was wearing an Australian Bush hat; the type with one side turned up. On it were miniature pins from different combat groups. I gave him one of my Little Bear pins and he promptly applied it in place. There were others too, who took time out from the real world and brought us some of its humor. Bob Hope, Phyllis Diller, Mel Torme, Ann Margaret, Joey Heatherton, James Garner, John Wayne, Joey

Heatherton, Danny Kaye, and Vicki Carr. Those were just a few. Did I mention Joey Heatherton?

There were clear hot days with a few clouds to see your shadow on, and days we flew on the deck under black monsoon skies. Flying just above the roads at high speeds, passing over the tops of Vietnamese civilians pedaling their bicycles, going about the everyday business of trying to survive in a war torn country, I often wondered whether they cared we were there. It seemed like rice and their family were the only things that mattered to them. Poor and simple people living off the land. How much did it matter to them who controlled their country? The rain would come, the rice would grow, and their world would not change. They would always be poor and simple people.

The reality of war was always brought back to me by the flights to the morgue at Tan Son Nhut loaded with stacks of body bags. Precious cargo entombed in a leatherette fabric. We flew these at night under the cover of darkness. Appropriate now that I recall. A dark, lone ship delivering sadness. At the landing pad, they would be hustled off into a gray quanson hut to be prepared for the long silent journey home. They were sons, fathers, or brothers, deprived from living the guarantee of life, justice and the pursuit of happiness. And for what? People like me.

What the hell, it was just another mission.

The Bear

It was only fitting that a company called the Little Bears would have a bear as a mascot. Bears are known all over the world for their fierceness, strength and courage. A white bear clutching a lightening bolt decorated the nose and sides of our aircraft.

On a scrounging mission to Nui Ba Den outside of Tay Ninh, Staff Sergeant Morales noticed that a Special Forces camp had a baby Malay Sun Bear. They are usually referred to as Asian Sun Bears because of a gold patch of fur on their chest. She was about three feet tall and mostly black with a gold covered snout. They had rescued it from an area full of mines and booby traps. The thought of it setting off one of those things and possibly dying a slow and agonizing death prompted them to bring her back to their compound. This variety of bear at full adulthood would reach only about four feet tall; the smallest of the eight bear species. Sergeant Morales called Little Bear flight operations to inform them of his discovery. It wasn't long before negotiations began. One great thing about having helicopters at your disposal was that you could take anything anywhere. The Special Forces camp was at the top of the mountain and needed a generator more than a pet bear. The swap was consummated and "Spooky" would become the mascot of A Company, 25th Aviation Battalion. After a full examination by a veterinarian in Saigon, she was dedicated as the company mascot by none other than General William Westmoreland himself. She bore the nickname of one of the finest pilots in our unit, Major Robert (Spook) Grundman who was killed flying a medevac mission a few months later.

Spooky had quite the personality. She would sometimes get free of her restraints and run amuck in the company area, scrounging around for food like most animals do. She ripped off the door of a small refrigerator one night and consumed all the liquid inside, mostly alcohol. By the time we caught up with her she had already destroyed a reel-to-reel tape deck and was working on the speakers. Believe me, there's nothing worse than a drunk bear with attitude!

She became somewhat of a celebrity around the camp. Even Charlton Heston stopped by on his tour to see her.

Spooky survived the four years the unit was in Vietnam. Arrangements were made with a zoo in Hawaii to receive her on our return back to Oahu, the 25th Infantry Divisions home base. She didn't survive the trip. An accidental overdose of sedatives and tranquilizers to help her tolerate the long flight back sadly ended her life.

Night Mission

I enjoyed flying. I wasn't actually *flying* the helicopter; I just hung out the side and watched the world slip by beneath. We flew without the benefit of sliding doors to seal out the weather. The doors could mean the death of us all if they became dislodged in combat and struck the ship. I did get my share of "stick" time in the pilot's seat. It was common practice among our pilots to teach the gunner and crew chief how to fly the helicopter. Perhaps it made them feel they were carrying a spare.

A door gunner is always on the alert for ground activity or aircraft sharing the sky. Nowhere we flew was ever safe from enemy fire or the possibility of colliding with another aircraft, but there were times when your mind slipped away and you forget for a moment where you were. Sometimes at night, flying into Tan Son Nhut, the lights below could have been any other city in any part of the world. It was a quick temporary escape from the realities of war. I could see the Big Dipper and know that someone somewhere else could see it too.

It was a simple reassuring fact another world existed, far away as it was. I had flown a lot of lone ship night missions to desolate firebases. The pilot would put us on a flight plan that kept us well above enemy fire. Blackness encompassed us. Darkness above and below with only the sound of the wind and the rotor blades. It would lure you to sleep until the automatic alarm in your body forced you to wake with one violent jerk. Sleep was a dream caught in a nightmare.

We once picked up a woman and her young daughter, both in need of medical attention. The girl was about ten. How frightening it must have been for them, being whisked up by strangers and lifted off the ground, flying for the first time, nothing to see but the vastness of a dark sky with the cold night air whipping through the ship. They clung to each other sitting on the jump seats occasionally used for passengers. Feelings were a hindrance in Vietnam. Thinking about anything but your job could get you and your crew killed. Compassion for their situation overcame me. I clicked the mike on my helmet to let the pilot know I was going to leave my gun to check on our passengers.

I unbuckled my safety belt and slipped on the seat next to them. Their wide eyes verified my suspicions. They were afraid and cold. Not knowing any Vietnamese, I handed them my field jacket to help them stay warm. The pilot's voice in my helmet asked me if I was up to date on my plague shots. Seems we were taking them in for treatment. Nothing like the thought of dying from a painful disease to cheer you up. I returned to my machine gun. After we arrived at the base hospital and dropped the pair off, it was the last I ever saw of them or my field jacket.

In a land far from my own home, I learned a simple lesson. Dress warmly; it's a dark, cold world outside.

First Kill

The war was all about body count. Statistics were constantly broadcast over the Armed Forces radio and printed in the *Stars and Stripes*. Nothing was a success unless you had a body count of some kind. It was normal after returning from a combat assault to discuss who had gotten the most kills that day. Usually, after a mission, the gunners would end up sitting in the enlisted men's beer hall at "our" table next to the jukebox. One table would become two, then three pushed together as the ships would return to base and we finished cleaning and inspecting our machine guns. A gunner's reputation was based on how well his guns operated. The M-60 was a machine and like any other machine, parts would wear, wear would lead to breakage, breakage to failure. In my entire tour, my machine guns never failed.

A mission involving a blocking force had me flying door gunner for the "C & C" ship. The Command and Control helicopter flew well above the on going operation and would coordinate ground and aircraft activity. Infantry units had been deployed to sweep through a large area suspected of housing Viet Cong troops. The flight of Little Bears flew back to the staging area and awaited word from our ship as to when and where they should drop off the remaining forces, when and if the first group was successful in flushing out any enemy. It wasn't long before we spotted three people exiting the tree line, in a hurry to cross an open area. They were heading for another clump of woods in the distance. That would give me plenty of time to nail all three. Unfortunately we were flying at approximately 3000 feet, about 1000 more feet than we normally fly to protect the command officers on board. I was told not to fire because they wanted to make sure these three running guys were not friendly troops. I kept thinking to myself that the officers in charge were wasting time. I knew that these guys running to beat hell were not just out jogging. I requested the pilot to give me a high-speed low-level run and I could bag all three once we got word to engage. Request denied because it would expose the brass on board to enemy fire. I was expected to hit these guys from our current altitude. Hit 'em? I could barely see them!

The word came and I was told to fire. Understand, we are flying about 100 knots at 3000 feet shooting at a running target. Usually I adjusted my firing by watching where the rounds struck the ground near the target. I could not make this out from our altitude so I just fired and fired all around these guys. First in front, then off to the side and finally behind them. It was like trying to drop a BB on top of a running ant from 20 feet up. I fired about 500 rounds at these people. I have to admit, I was feeling pretty incompetent. One of the running guys must have felt sorry for me and ran under a falling bullet. He slowed down and came to rest in a sitting position at the side of a bomb crater. The other two made it to cover in a small clump of trees. We circled the area until the grunts were able to go in.

Once the area was declared secure, we dropped to ground level to search for the wounded guy. We had just come around the edge of a crater when I saw him sitting there, not moving. I swung the machine gun around in his direction just before the commander yelled at me not to fire, he wanted to take him alive. It was too late. After the grunts got over to him, we landed nearby and they loaded his body in our ship. He was definitely VC with ammo, grenades, food and other supplies secured to his belt. After searching him for ID and any information he may have been carrying we took his body over to the morgue at our base camp.

I never considered myself to be a violent person but I just tried to eliminate three people. It felt like I was at an amusement park shooting gallery. I was happy to win a prize. On the way back in, I looked at this guy and searched myself for feelings. There were none. The U.S. Army had done its job well.

I was now a killer.

Dust-off

Dust-off was the term for a Medevac mission. All helicopters monitored a special radio frequency that would allow the closest one to respond. Sometimes ground troops would be under fire, so getting in and out for the pick up could prove very exciting. If the VC knew a helicopter was on the way, they would hold off a little just to get a chance at knocking us out. It varied between mortars, rocket grenades, small arms fire or a combination of any of these.

We once landed a few meters behind some U.S. ground forces pinned down by heavy automatic weapons fire coming from a wooded area. They were firing from a prone position. I let off about 500 rounds over their heads into the tree line. I fired straight tracer rounds that light up as they come out of the barrel. That's all I ever loaded in my machine guns. They glowed when they came at you. Sometimes just scaring the shit out of someone was as good as hitting them. I was having a good time until I heard the explosive *kaboom* of the first mortar hit near our position. The pilots hung in there long enough for the wounded guy to be put on board. I remember the soldiers loading their buddy and giving me the big thumbs up. Made me feel good. War is not about killing the enemy as much as it is about saving your own guys.

The wounded were always serious, sometimes already dead. Their blood would create rivers that flowed under my seat and were sucked out, atomizing in front of me as it collided into the wash of the rotor blades.

I had more respect for the medics than for anyone else in the war. An Armored Personnel Carrier (APC) struck a mine, severely injuring one soldier. Over the noise of the rotor blades, I could hear the medic screaming, frantically trying to save the kid's life. I looked at the guy as they loaded him on board and realized the shinny white object protruding from his distorted body was a rib. I was sure he was dead. As he lay on his back the blood formed pools in his eye sockets that filled and overflowed, causing dark red streams across his face. The medic would not give up and worked on him until we landed at the base hospital.

I tried to never look at the dead or wounded. That kept me apart from them. This job had no place for feelings and the ones you developed were buried so deep, they would not surface for years. The best people to have with you were stone people. I look back now and think someone else fought this war, not me. War will change you. We were trained well. Some of us came back home cold, reckless and without feeling. We were different from other people and suffered a silent loneliness. A fellow vet put it all in perspective when he asked, "How do you get the Genie back in the bottle?"

"Little Bear" pocket patch

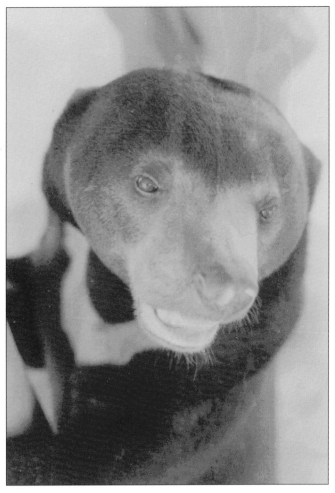

"Spooky"

Loading up wounded

Pulling troops out of the "Iron Triangle"

Diamondheads

The "B" Company "Diamondheads" were the teeth of the 25th Aviation Battalion. During the time I was in Vietnam, they consisted of eight C-Model Hueys, two small observation helicopters and a couple of small fixed wing aircraft.

The C-Models did not have the capacity of our troop-carrying ships. They were a shorter version and served as gun ships. Artillery for most of these helicopters was a set of flex-guns mounted on each side of the ship and a 40-MM grenade launcher secured under the nose. The flex guns were basically two M-60 machine guns mounted on top of each other. The pilot controlled the firing. They also flew with a gunner and crew chief. The really bad ships packed 48 rockets and a grenade launcher or anything else they could mount on it. The rockets were usually a combination of HE (high explosive) or WP (White Phosphorus). They were called "Hogs." If you ever saw one trying to lift off, you would understand how they picked up this unflattering nickname. Loaded to capacity on take off, and dragging the front tips of the skids along the ground, it looked like some plump old Kentucky sow rooting for food.

The Diamondheads' main mission was attack support for the 25th Division's infantry, armor and mechanized units. They also flew as flare dropping ships and escort for the Medevac ships. This was the group that developed the use of the mini-gun as firepower on Huey gunships.

The mini-gun was a rotating multi-barrel mounted machine gun that could fire about 6000 rounds of ammo a minute. Watching one of these things in action was an awesome sight. Rounds spewed out of the barrels with a *braap* sound, and a short stream of light resembling a laser beam spat from it. It fired 4 and 1 (four regular and one tracer round) linked together. Coming out of the guns, they all looked red to me.

These guys were constantly in the face of the enemy. Flying into hot LZs seemed a little safer when they were around.

The unit served in 12 campaigns, receiving two Valorous Unit Awards, two Meritorious Unit Commendations and a Presidential Unit Citation. Their pilots and crews collected every medal in the book save for the Medal of Honor. Bravery and heroism had its price. The spirits of twenty-six young men now fly close support over the military graveyards of a thankless nation.

VIP Platoon

The VIP flight platoon had the four nicest
looking UH-1D helicopters in the company. They were
polished, fully equipped with the latest radio
technology, and sprouted two long radio whip antennas
from their skids. Their crews were required to wear
freshly starched fatigues daily. They flew above the
action and directed combat operations. These were also
the Hueys that chauffeured dignitaries or visiting
celebrities. Their ships looked like well-groomed
Cadillacs opposed to our spottily patched Fords. Not
that they didn't get their share of combat, though. My
good buddy Mike King flew as gunner specifically for a
commanding general. Mike told me about flying
missions with this guy and how the troops nicknamed

67

him "the Butcher of the Pineapple Fields." This general constantly sought out the enemy even if it meant flying on the deck (just off the ground). They were so successful at flushing out VC, Mike was one of the few door gunners promoted to sergeant and ended up with over 100 confirmed kills.

On a combat assault, I had seen his helicopter swoop down from its high observation position and join in the battle. The general was hanging out the Huey dropping hand grenades on a group of North Vietnamese Regulars we had caught by surprise. We were shot up pretty badly, but the "Old Man" wasn't about to let them get off easily.

One day Mike's ship was exploring for possible areas to launch a search and destroy operation when they spotted a weaponless guy riding a bicycle down a path bordering the woods. The general wanted to question this individual and ordered the pilot to drop from his 2500-foot altitude, buzz this guy and check him out. The low flyby didn't slow him down. Mike let off a few rounds in front of the bicycle to encourage him to stop. No go. This guy kept pedaling along, ignoring the circling ship. I don't know how it is in any other army, but it really pisses off generals when they don't get their way. He was steaming. He pulled his .45 pistol out of its holster and ordered the ship to land in front of his athletic foe. As soon as the ship hit the deck, out popped the general. It was now time for our blistering bicyclist to vacate his vehicle and run off into the nearby woods. The general trailed slightly behind waving his .45 and yelled for his prey to abandon his effortless flight.

Now you can only imagine what was going through the pilots' heads when they saw their commander disappear into the congested undergrowth. There's something about hanging around an open area known to be infested with heavily armed enemy troops that tends to make everyone edgy. How do you think it would have looked if they reported back to base they had "lost the general"? Both gunners scanned the area hoping to see signs of the returning pursuer while the Aircraft Commander kept the rotor blades spinning at a high rate of speed to help expedite take off if or when it was required. The general finally broke free from the encasing foliage even madder than when he entered. It seemed our cycling buddy had eluded the hunter and soon would be telling fellow comrades about his daring deed.

Frustrated beyond all comprehension, the general took aim at the captured vehicle with his .45 automatic, and blew out both tires. He then proceeded to bounce up and down on the spokes of the wheels, dislodging and reducing them to twisted lengths of wire.

Satisfied it would never be of use to anyone again, he reentered the ship and ordered it back to camp.

No one said a word.

Eagle Flights

Vietnam was your basic hit-and-run, hide-and-seek, war. We could not fight what we could not see. The Viet Cong tactics had been refined by years of fighting the French and Japanese. New search and destroy missions by U.S. troops tried to cope with this style of guerrilla warfare

Eagle Flights combined air-mobile units and heavily armed infantry. The idea was simple, one troop carrying helicopter flying low and slow, would create an inviting target for enemy snipers. Rumor had it a bounty had been placed on helicopters and door gunners. The number of bullet holes our Hueys managed to collect served to confirm this. I once heard a story about a ship returning from a mission with an

71

arrow stuck in the tail boom. Getting the enemy to fire on was never a real problem.

Two gun ships tailed the lone Huey. Once the decoy drew fire, the gun ships would mark the area and supply cover fire as it joined the flight of other ships out of sight from the unsuspecting attackers. They were also loaded with heavily armed infantry troops. Linked up, the decoy ship lead the flight and all troops were dropped off in an effort to surprise, destroy and pretty much flatten anything in the immediate area.

The first time we tried this operation, I was gunner on the decoy ship that lead the assault. Hours went by. We flew around the countryside, our eyes straining for signs of enemy activity. I hoped none of the infantry guys got air sick and barffed all over our ship. Finally it happened. Somebody on the ground with an automatic weapon fired a burst at us. We had the procedure down. The two gun ships flew a search pattern and off we went to bring back the troops and lead the attacking force in. Flying low and fast over the jungle gave us the advantage of surprise. We came back with our ten helicopters and approximately seventy heavily armed troops and landed in the middle of four hundred North Vietnamese Regulars.

Big surprise for everyone. Our machine guns fired off thousands of rounds to protect the unloading troops. People scattered in all directions. The North Vietnamese Army was using this piece of real estate as a resting area and was caught off guard. However, they were heavily armed, dug in and well dispersed. One of the NVA soldiers was set up inside the dirt mound of a rice paddy. He had a slot protected by two short pieces of logs tied together with a rope. He pushed the logs apart to fire at me, and then pulled on the rope to close the logs. I figured he must have had an old style rifle because he fired only one shot at a time. Unfortunately for him, the game ended abruptly. From inside the helicopter, I could hear the unmistakable sound of a .45 automatic pistol going off. All ten helicopters were struck by enemy fire. We were barely able to leave the LZ and limped over to a secure open area to check our damage. Of the ten ships, seven were damaged so badly we had to leave them to be extracted later. My ship received multiple hits, including one a couple of feet to my left. I was sure it was from my dug-in buddy. The windshield had several .45 caliber bullet holes, compliments of the pilot. There is no way to fire a machine gun directly in front of a helicopter. Door mounted machine guns had built in stops to prevent the gunner from accidentally shooting the pilot in the event of a sudden maneuver. The pilot that day, a Warrant Officer, was an Italian guy from New Jersey named Muccioli. Nothing fazed him. The enemy knew where we were vulnerable. Some guy popped up directly in front of our helicopter and before he could fire at us, the pilot drew his pistol and let off five rounds right through the Plexiglas windshield. I guess that pop up guy never met anyone from New Jersey before.

The damage to 626 was minor, a few bullets passed through the tail boom without hitting anything important. It added a few more patches to our collection and gave us another story to tell. Kind of like showing your buddies old scars. What was left of our flight headed back to Cu-Chi at full speed to refuel and re-arm. We wanted to get back into this battle. The rest of the ships would either be repaired in the field or later sling loaded and hauled back to base. We would hook up with another aviation unit to await new orders.

Our three remaining ships arrived at the refueling area at the same time. Rows of tanker trucks held thousands of gallons of JP-4 to top us off. Ammo was stacked in cases near by. On the ground, my first job was to unlatch the pilot's door on my side and slide back his seat's left side armor plate. This would enable him to exit in a hurry if necessary.

I ran for the stacks of linked ammo and Jerry made for the fuel truck and grabbed the hose. He soon had the nozzle shoved into the side of the ship. I was pulling the ammo out of their tin containers to link them up with mine when I noticed the crew chief from the ship behind us dancing around and beating on the side of his helicopter. Everyone's adrenaline was maxing out. The rotor wash from the main blades blew up dirt, whipping it against our face and into our eyes. The high winding turbine engines of our three Hueys filled the air with sounds of popping rotor blades.

I suddenly realized what was happening to the ship ten feet behind us. Flames whooshed out of the fuel inlet. A spark must have set off the fuel vapor and the crew chief was frantically trying to beat it out. All I could see was his ship exploding and setting off all the fuel-trucks and us along with them. Fear would have been a wasted emotion. In a moment, the ordeal was over. The flame was extinguished, leaving another memory for late night reviewing.

The day ended with us picking up the embattled ground forces and heading back to camp. We suffered no casualties. The ground troops had several but overall the operation was a success. It was that day we picked up the nickname "Lucky Little Bears."

Flying Arvins

Flying leaflet-dropping missions seemed to me a waste of good aviation fuel and time. A program titled Cu Hoi (Open Arms) was developed. The object was to convince any Viet Cong to surrender into the arms of the South Vietnamese Army. The Army of the Republic of Vietnam soldiers were referred to as "Arvins" among the U.S. troops. The surrendering VCs were promised good treatment, meals and medical attention if needed. Following rehabilitation, they would be drafted into the South Vietnamese Army to fight against their former cohorts. We dropped leaflets from our ship containing that information and a slip the surrendering Viet Cong could hand to his captors guaranteeing him these rewards. Life for these troops underground in tunnel complexes lacked luxuries. Picking up haggard, underweight prisoners showed the strength of their conviction in fighting their war.

What usually happened is after the surrendering individual was well fed and healthy, he would escape or desert and return to his old unit.

The last time I tossed leaflets out the door, I ended up staring at twenty rounds of automatic weapons fire getting ready to cross the underside of my ship. The tracers glowed orange. I thought for sure that we would collect a few. I popped a white smoke grenade and launched it out the door to mark the location. Probably made some VC irate because we littered up his jungle. The pilot put the ship into a turn so tight; I was starring straight down at the treetops. In awe I watched condensation streaming off the tips of the rotor blades. We circled back to find the shooter, but like most other attackers, he melted back into the dense woods.

On one occasion, while landing a company of Arvins into an LZ, the last soldier to exit turned and rolled a live grenade under one of our Hueys. It went off wounding the gunner, but not before he unleashed enough rounds into the guy to put him on the permanently disabled list. He turned out to be one of those "reformed" Viet Cong individuals.

Flying Arvin troops made me nervous. As soon as young men turned 18, they were drafted into the South Vietnamese Army. Anyone not in the service and of age was considered to be Viet Cong. It did not matter what religious order you belonged to, or if you were a conscientious objector. Your butt was drafted. Some of these young guys did not fair well once they got into a hot LZ. I understand fear. I saw it hit a friend when we were caught in a mortar attack with nowhere to hide. We dropped to the ground and lay flat on our stomachs. I could hear him sobbing and calling for his mother while the rounds detonated around us. We escaped the ordeal without injury. There was never a need to repeat this incident to anyone. War without fear is a dangerous thing.

In one of these hot situations, two Arvin troops refused to exit the helicopter with their squad. The longer we were in the zone, the more we were exposed to enemy fire. Bishop, the gunner, a sturdy built guy from Detroit, had to physically grab these guys and toss them out. He swore later that he did not realize his ship was twenty feet off the ground. They both survived with broken legs and had to be evacuated. They got their way out temporarily.

Like any other army, you have your good and bad soldiers. The Arvins fought bravely and suffered heavy losses going against the North Vietnamese Army. They did have their share of victories. They fought the enemy without U.S. help during the last years of the war. Many people conceded a different ending might have taken place.

Sounded kind of funny when Bishop told me about flinging those two guys out of the Huey later at the EM club. I commented to him that of all the ships on the mission that day, he was the only one actually "flying Arvins." He laughed so hard he spit out his beer and farted at the same time. War brings out a cold humor in people who fight.

Best Friend

It was one of the cooler days that month,
somewhere in the low 90s. Jerry was repainting the
inside deck of 626 and I managed to get out of the
company area before someone realized I was roaming
around without any duties. Even though officers in
Vietnam overlooked some formalities, it was still the
U.S. Army, where anyone caught with nothing to do
would be guaranteed some menial time-consuming
task.

Well into my second year, I discovered no one
questioned a member of a flight crew walking out to the
airfield with a flight helmet in one hand and a flak vest
in the other. Nobody had regular days off in this war

zone, so it was up to the individual to secure them whenever he could.

A lot of guys had nicknames painted on the side of their flight helmets. To grunts, jumping in and out of Hueys, all door gunners looked alike. Battered fatigues, gray flak vest and a faded green flight helmet scarred from many harsh introductions to other parts of the helicopter. With one of its two face shields pulled down, nobody could tell who was inside.

I decided I would no longer be anonymous. While Jerry was busy with a half gallon of battleship gray paint, I scrounged around for some type of instrument to scribble a name on my helmet. The only real brushes available were five inches wide and one inch thick, great for painting floors of a Huey, but a little tough for fine detail writing. I yanked a couple of dried grass stocks out of the ground. They were stiff, long and could support a fair amount of paint. In my best handwriting, I carefully wrote out, "Frisco Kid." I was raised in San Francisco. How clever! I had combined my nickname with my hometown. The common question about "Where you from?" could now be answered before it was asked.

Sitting at a forward artillery support base, with ten ships and a load of infantry one day, my helmet would prompt one of the grunts to ask if I was from California. I gave him my "Dumb shit, you don't know San Francisco is in California" look. The green and black nametag above his right pocket read "Bettinger." Wrapped in bandoleers of machine gun bullets and holding an M-60, he was about six feet tall. He said he was from California too. "LA." This guy was with a group of "Wolfhounds" (infantry company nickname) we were waiting to take on an assault. This company had fought fierce battles and taken heavy losses at times. I'd picked up many of their wounded. I don't think any other company in our division received as much respect as these guys. It turns out Bettinger's first name was John. He asked me a lot of questions about door gunning. I told him it sure beat hacking away in the bush. To me, flying was the best thing going. To most grunts, they just thought we sniffed a little too much aviation fuel.

One thing about these fire support bases, they usually had local villagers trying to sell something. When a little girl about 14 walked up to our ship with a basket of Orange Crush soda on ice, I bought two and gave one to John. We continued to talk until the word came down to crank up. Ten minutes later, in the LZ, I covered John and his buddies as they disappeared into the thick foliage of the Vietnamese jungle. A few weeks later, this same guy jumped into my Huey as we prepared to leave base for another search and destroy mission.

John mentioned he volunteered for assignment to A Company to become a Little Bear door gunner. It was then I knew he was an all-right guy. Once again, after landing in some other nameless LZ, I watched as he disappeared into the woods with his squad. This time, I wished him luck.

One night, a month or so later, I was sitting at my desk by my cot. It was nothing more than an eight by twelve inch, piece of thin pine wood from an ammo box nailed to and supported by the side of the hooch.

It was about 2100 when a truck loaded with loud partying GIs stopped just outside the door. A moment later, two laughing, mostly inebriated guys kicked open the hooch door. Supported between the two of them hung a slack body. "We brought your new gunner!" The new gunner looked pretty pale. The smell of marijuana followed the three in like a vapor trail. He must have been quite a guy. Nobody gets a going away party like that unless he's well respected.

They tossed his limp body on an end bunk and departed. It was the machine gunner from the Wolfhounds. Shortly after John received his orders to transfer to our company, his sergeant major gave him a send off party. Having already been wounded twice, Bettinger was the longest-surviving enlisted man in his platoon. Sergeant Major Ruttledge then delivered John to our head sergeant's hooch with the order "not to fuck with Bettinger" or he would come back and kick his ass. Now that's what I call respect!

John and I became great friends and together we found a multitude of ways to relieve the occasional boredom of Vietnam. One quiet evening, after taking advantage of some natural herbal attitude enhancers, we found ourselves passing the Officers Club.

The officers were having one of their occasional mixed social gatherings. To John and me, it sounded a little dull. We decided to liven it up a little. I brought back a few packs of firecrackers from my last R & R visit to Taiwan and felt this would be the perfect opportunity to enjoy them. The only nice surface appeared to be at front door of the Officer's Club.

Being fairly enhanced, we planned to light off all the firecrackers, yell, "Attack, attack!" jump into the nearest bunker and watch what transpired.

I have to admit Chinese sure know how to make fireworks. Every one of those little suckers went off. The noise bounced off the walls of that club and landed in the company area fifty yards away. Secure in our box seats, we awaited the mass exodus. Nothing. No scrambling officers, no hysterical nurses, the band played on. A loud voice from inside the club declared, "Its just Lazzarini and Bettinger. They're hiding in the bunker."

What a terrible waste of some very nice fireworks.

If someone predicted that two years later we would be roommates, living in Los Angeles, smoking dope, chasing women and playing the Rolling Stones so loud on the stereo the neighbors would constantly bang the apartment walls, I probably would have believed them. Two years later, it became true.

John is still one of my best friends.

Spook Missions

Captain Kulhavi, now promoted, approached me one day to say he would be going on a one-ship mission. This would be a little different from the rest and he wanted to handpick his crew. For the crew chief he had requested Dave Budde. Dave and I flew together occasionally and shared the same hooch. He had this great reel-to-reel tape system on which he constantly played Johnny River's "Rewind" album. I liked it so much, when I returned to the states, I purchased the 8-track tape to play in my new 1968 AMX.

Dave was an unshakable guy. He used to say that he was going to get himself a Silver Star (Military decoration) some day. I believed him. I'd seen him a little unraveled only once. He had just come back from a medevac mission involving a civilian passenger bus going down a two-lane highway we called Route One. The VC planted high explosive mines that tripped only when contacted by a heavy vehicle such as a tank or APC. Unfortunately, a bus full of women, kids and old men weighed enough to set it off.

Transportation was hard to get so these buses were usually packed. Dave had returned to base camp after making multiple runs to a local hospital. As he approached me in our hooch, I could tell by his manner and the look in his eyes that something was not right. He went on to tell me about the evac. By the time he got to the scene, the dead had been separated from the wounded. Some people were moaning, some stunned in deep shock. Looking for the most serious to load first, he spotted a young girl about 12, wearing those traditional black pajama outfits. She was on the ground, crying and clutching her bleeding leg. She had been struck by a flying piece of metal from the explosion. He bent down to pick her up and was carrying her over to the Huey when he felt something fall on his foot. It was one of the young girl's legs. The last clinging piece of flesh had surrendered to its weight. It had been completely severed from just below her hip. This was one of those experiences you need to tell someone about to get it out of your mind. We shared his agony.

For the gunner, John said he had volunteered me. The only other thing he mentioned was to leave all personal ID's, dog tags, wallet or anything with a U.S. insignia on it, at base. We picked up an unmarked black Huey somewhere in the boonies. We did this quite a few times. Years later back in the states having dinner with him, some friends and my wife Arlene, I asked, "John, did you take me along on these missions because you liked me or because you didn't like me?"

These types of missions were referred to as "FOB" missions (fly over the border). Usually Cambodia. Most of the time we flew in LRRPs, Long-Range Reconnaissance Patrols, or guys dressed in camouflage gear I assumed to be assassination teams. I never asked who they were and no one ever told me. We stood by close to the border to retrieve them in a hurry if needed.

On another mission, we flew a black Huey with a huge tank of liquid in it; took up most the cargo area of the ship. It had water pipes extending out on both sides and looked like crop dusting equipment. Our mission that day was to spray a large rice paddy in Cambodia. It supplied food for the North Vietnamese Army when they came down the Ho Chi Mhin Trail to enter Vietnam. We made pass upon pass, long, low runs, spraying the stuff, up and back, up and back. The ship came manned with two guys to operate the thing. Jerry and I were making bets how long it would be before one of them heaved his breakfast. Hell, I didn't care; this wasn't even my Huey! Then a little flash caught my eye. I wasn't sure at first, but on the next pass, I saw it again. There was a bunker just on the rim of the paddy. Every time we made a pass, someone inside was taking a shot at us. He must have been short on ammo because he fired one round at a time, plus, he was a piss poor shot! I informed the pilot. We held off making runs and within ten minutes I saw this thing go up in a glowing orange and black cloud of smoke. Seems somebody else was not supposed to be there too. We continued till we ran out of liquid then headed back across the boarder to pick up our own ship.

This was the first mission I was involved with in Operation Ranch Hand and, you guessed it, my first experience with Agent Orange.

The Cards

The best thing happening in Vietnam? Mail call twice a day. It was always nice to hear from someone even if I never took too much time to respond back. I mean, what can you tell the folks back home about your day? It would have to go something like this.

Hi folks:
Looks like a great day today. Got up early because of a mortar attack. This time they nailed the generators for the hot water showers. At least they did not hit the beer hall. HA HA! Went over to the mess hall for some powdered eggs and recombined milk. Lucky for me I

spotted the cockroach legs deep-fried with the bacon. Might have been something else. They got quite a collection of bugs over here. The locals just pull heads and legs off live ones and pop them in their mouths. I'm down 15 pounds and don't eat much anyway. Happy to say my foot rot is not getting worse. Found out the annoying itch I have is just crabs and nothing contagious.

I got the package you sent to help me celebrate my 20th birthday. The fresh fruit and salami was a big hit with the guys I shared them with. We fired up a couple of fat ones and ate everything in one sitting.

Must be about 115 outside. We were afraid it might get hot today. Thank God the weather cooled off.

I had a great time on my R & R to Bangkok. Met this really nice hooker and she showed me around town. Did you know the Government regulates them? I tell you it's the best buy you can get for only twelve bucks a night! Spent the entire week hanging out with her. She's great. Too bad they haven't legalized prostitution in the States. I'm all for it!

We're getting ready to go out on a big assault today. We will be picking up about 100 grunts and dropping them off in the Hobo Woods. It's that place I wrote to you about last week where we lost three ships going in. Maybe today I can get me a couple more gooks to make up for it. I'm still behind Sgt. Kellogg for most kills but catching up fast.

Have to make this short cause I have to re-arm the Huey with smoke grenades and ammo.

Will write again soon.

Your loving son

Needless to say, I didn't write home a lot.

Early in December of 1966, I received a Christmas card from a girl whose name was not familiar. The card was signed with no note. I noticed she misspelled my last name on the envelope. It has two Z's in it and only one had been used. I dropped it in my tin footlocker made from the finest beer cans the local Vietnamese could find and forgot about it. The next mail call, I received a few more cards from people I did not know wishing me a Merry Christmas; again missing a Z in my last name. A note in one of the cards explained. A San Francisco radio station, KSFO, compiled a list of local service men and gave them out to any one that wanted to send a card. I must have received 100 Christmas cards. They were from all sorts of people, young and old. I received hand made cards from kids in elementary schools and store-bought ones from elderly people living in downtown hotel rooms. Some just signed their names and others wrote to tell me about their families and thoughts. I was so taken by their generosity; I purchased a box of Christmas cards at the P.X. and wrote each one of them to thank them.

I kept in touch with a few for a while. To some of the elementary schoolboys I sent black and green shoulder patches from my division and sets of gunner's wings.

Someone sent a bumper sticker from the radio station sponsoring the mailing. I stuck it on the tail of 626. It read, "KSFO Loves You!" I gathered up a few friends and we all stood underneath it while one of my buddies snapped a shot. I made a few copies and sent one to the radio station with a thank-you note. I still have the picture. The bumper sticker had to go when someone pointed out it glowed in the dark and made a real nice target.

I saved the Christmas cards for over thirty years in a clear plastic bag. They now reside in a special album of their own.

It amazes me to think that some of the young people who sent those cards are now twice the age I was when I received them. Who said time travel is impossible?

Black Virgin Mountain

Diamondhead gunship

Loading up for a combat assault

Jerry checking out damage to 626

30-Day Leave

It was the final two months of my first tour when I started to have issues about going back to the States. Part of me wanted to leave Vietnam and the other part wanted to stay. The army life in Vietnam was far removed from the army life in the world. I was trained as a soldier and to me it did not make much sense not using those skills. Service life back in the USA would mean countless inspections, snappy uniforms, and being militarily correct. Out in the war, those things did not mean shit. No one cared about the polish on your boots as long as it did not affect your ability under fire. I cannot recall a single instance when some VC did not shoot at me because he was so impressed by my shiny boots or the creases in my fatigues. Being married or having a steady girlfriend would have made my final decision easier. That was not the case. In a strange way, I was living a great adventure. For women it would be giving birth, for men it was going to war.

In Vietnam I was living on the edge, day-to-day with people I could really trust. Not just with money or possessions but with my life. There was no gray. Black and white were the dominant colors of the day. You did your job or you didn't. No excuses, no whining, rarely a second chance. There were people I did not care for, did not need or had to befriend, but they all had my respect. War was a great expediter. It weeds out the bad quickly and effectively. You did not have to be John Wayne or Sergeant York; you just had to be yourself, do your job. Your buddies came first; the war was a mere hindrance. Like many others, I was there for them, not the country of Vietnam.

I signed up for another six months in country. It turned into nine.

I decided not to tell anyone I was coming home on a 30-day leave. One reason was for the sheer surprise of it all. The other was to avoid the questions of "Why?" a little longer.

It was 6:00 p.m. when I stepped off the plane at San Francisco International Airport. I had not made arrangements for anyone to pick me up. This was a *surprise*. I called the father of one of my closest friends. He had always treated me like his own son. My family life before the service was less than perfect, and Len Miller had the respect I would have gladly given to my real father. I was on my second stepfather when I met him. His son Dan and I went through junior high and high school together. Len to me was the father of all fathers. I was 15 when he took his son and me to see my first Major League baseball game, the Giants versus Dodgers. The Giants came in second that day, 5 to 7. I was envious of the relationship the father and son had with each other. That envy carries through to this day. This was the kind of dad who bought a new 1965 Pontiac GTO and let his 18-year-old son drive it. While I was in Vietnam not writing letters to many people, Len called the American Red Cross, said he was my father and wanted to know how I was. My First Sergeant tracked me down and gave me hell for not writing to my family.

Waiting at the airport, I treated myself to a T-bone steak and the first glass of real milk I had in almost a year. There was no such thing as fresh cow's milk in Vietnam at that time. If there was, it never trickled down to us little people.

Len greeted me with great warmth and genuine excitement. His death wish comment after I told him I was returning to Vietnam would be the first of many I heard during my visit. He drove me home to an apartment building where my family rented a third floor unit. As I made my way up the flights of stairs, I felt the tension building up inside me. I had not seen my stepfather's truck in the carport, so I wouldn't have to deal with him. He was the main reason I left home the day after I graduated from high school. It was a Friday night and my high school age sister and brother were out on dates. My echoing knock on the door was greeted by the barking reply of our dog Luke. He was a small, long red hair mutt, but a great dog all the same. My mother was trying to hold back Luke when she opened the door. She was bent over trying to restrain him and looked up to see who the visitor was the same time I said, "Surprise!" She was a small woman, with bright red hair, who spent most of her life waiting on people in restaurants. Later she became the hostess known as "Red" or "Edie" at one of the most famous restaurants in San Francisco: Scoma's at Fisherman's Wharf. She lost her personal war with cancer before her 57th birthday.

I spent a lot of time driving around alone in my 1959 Fiat Spider. I had resurrected it from the auto wreckers, owned by my real father in San Francisco. I missed driving more than anything. While I was on one of my R & R's in Taiwan, I gave the cabdriver 50 bucks to let me drive his car! I took a lot of trips along the coast running from San Francisco to Santa Cruz. With the top down and the wind blowing through my hair, it was like flying shotgun. The war was half a world away, but still with me. Most of my high school buddies were attending distant colleges or in the military. I was about the only one serving in Vietnam. One surprise was an invitation to speak at the high school my sister and brother attended. San Carlos High School was also the same school from which I graduated in 1964.

It was in January of 1967 and a lot of the senior boys were turning draft age. The students appreciated a closer look at the war from the perspective of someone who'd been there. My only regret was I had no visual aids to offer them during my appearances. I tried to be as non-political as I could and gave them straight answers. I picked up a camera during my second tour and shot about 300 slides. After my discharge from the army in 1968, I again returned to the same school, but this time better prepared.

In 1969 over 540,000 men served in Vietnam. Some were the same kids I had spoken to the year before.

And then it was time.

My good friend Mike Kuhlman drove me to Oakland Naval Base where arrangements were made for my return back to Vietnam. I spent the last night back in the states trying to remember everything I had done in the last thirty days. I recalled them all. I was joined by hundreds of other young GIs going over for their first tour of duty. We were all on military flights for the next thirty hours or so. They were fresh out of Advanced Infantry Training and inoculated for plague, typhus, polio, flu, cholera, smallpox, yellow fever and typhoid. Their dark green fatigues would soon fade from the hot sun of Vietnam and shred from a multitude of encounters with jungle undergrowth. Vietnamese women would launder them in rice paddy water and beat them with thick palm leaves. Their fatigues would absorb the odor of the country. Poor sanitary conditions would introduce them to crabs, boils, ringworm and jungle rot. They were young men leaving with thoughts of valor and heroism only to return filled with coagulants and painkillers.

Over 58,000 men would die and 300,000 would be wounded by the time the U.S. pulled out of Vietnam. Sixty-one percent of the men killed in action were 21 or younger.

At 20 years old, I was going back to give the VC another shot at me.

Slick Humor

Even in a war zone, things happened that made you laugh. Most of the humorous incidents involved ground troops trying to get off the Huey in a hurry. The longer they hesitated, the more time it gave the enemy to hit us with small arms fire, mortars, or rocket launchers. You only need to witness one ship burning in an LZ to understand the meaning of expedient exits.

We usually flew troop insertions with 8-10 helicopters flying in a staggered formation. It was tight grouping and all gunners cross-fired with another ship to provide protective cover for the unloading grunts and us. We landed in line and took off as a group.

The first guys out of the Huey had a tendency to stand on the helicopter landing skids prior to touching down. If the surface looked muddy or was covered in water, the pilots kept the ship hovering a foot or two off the ground. Pilots found out earlier, that landing in the mud would sometimes get the skids sucked in and we could have a problem making an exit. Not knowing the depth of the water or what was underneath could prove to be deadly.

We were dropping a company of infantry in an area full of rice paddies. I noticed the machine gunner in the squad had inched his way over to the door. He had his M-60 machine locked in a white knuckled grip with bandoleers of ammo wrapped around his body. He was a short stocky guy, about five foot three or four. He looked wound a little tight and definitely wanted off the ship as soon as possible. The pilot brought us to a level hovering position about a foot above the paddy. I was checking out a distant wooded area for any activity when this guy left the ship. In an instant there was a scramble of activity in the Huey. The only visible object of the gunner who leaped out of the ship was his helmet bobbing on top of the water. The rice paddy must have been four or five feet deep! With all the weight this guy was carrying, he went completely under and out of sight. Two of his buddies reached down and pulled him to the surface. He had this wild-eyed look on his face and was coughing and spitting out pieces of rice stalks. I had to turn away because I didn't want him to see the tears coming out of my eyes from laughing so hard. He might have swung that '60 around.

I flew with some extremely skilled crew chiefs. These were the guys who maintained the ships and acted as the door gunner on the other side once their ships were airborne. On many occasions, after flying all day, they spent even more time performing scheduled maintenance or repairs once we got back to base.

Specialist Walker was from Tennessee. His southern drawl was enhanced by his ability to spread two syllable words into four. Nothing, and I mean nothing, ever excited this guy. I had a feeling he was one of those back-hill guys. So far back they needed to pump in sunshine. He knew his helicopters though. Every now and then, I would fly as a temporary gunner on another ship. The usual guy being not available due to leave, R & R, wounds, death or transfer.

Flying during the rainy season had its own disadvantages. The big thing was we got cold and wet. Loading troops in and out of muddy fields caked the inside of our ship with a layer of sticky red clay. The sky was an ominous black. The cold wind ripped through the ship making everyone on board miserable and edgy. At times like this, we found very little to laugh about. Once again in a mud-covered LZ, the Little Bears were dropping off infantry. I was flying in Walker's ship. The wind had been blowing at a pretty good pace jostling the Hueys around as we tried to land. Just before we set down a sudden gust joggled our ship. A soldier exiting on Walker's side fell face down in the mud and was stretched out under us as we started to land. The skids caught him on the back of his legs and were pushing him into the muck. The only person who saw this was Walker. I had my headset on and could hear his Tennessee voice slowly spread out the announcement, "Sir, you might want to pick us up a bit. We're squashing some feller."

Lucky for the grunt, the mud was soft and he sustained no injuries. I'm sure he still talks about the day a Huey landed on him.

Sometimes, our own coolness got us into trouble. One of my gunner buddies, a Texas boy named Hicks, flew to Saigon on a Huey to pick up some replacements for the base hospital. They were all female nurses. It wasn't that often we would come in close contact with any round-eyed women, so he decided to go to extra lengths to insure their safety. Hicks was one of the gunners who wore the monkey-strap harnesses. After the women were on board, he exited his side of the ship to make sure they all had their seat belts tightened. It was common practice to stand on top of the helicopter skids, for some extra height. He was too busy reaching over the ladies laps to make sure their seat belts were secure to notice his radio helmet had disconnected. He was flashing a big old southern boy smile and being as doggone helpful as he could be. Satisfied and happy that the ladies were secure and comfortable, he stepped off the skid to return to his perch behind the machine gun and down he went. With no radio communication with the other members of the crew, he was unaware the AC had brought us to a hover about ten feet off the ground. The pilots found out his plight by a call from the flight tower informing them they had a gunner hanging from the skids. Luckily for Hicks he had on that strap. He was swinging, hollering, arms and legs flapping, like some large, green bait on the end of a fishing line. I would try to convince him of trying this clever tactic out on our next search and destroy mission to draw enemy fire. I told him we could call it, "trolling for Charlie." From his two-word response, I got the feeling he did not like that idea.

Emergency Re-supply

War never rests, takes a break or goes out for a pee. It was not uncommon to be awakened in the middle of the night and find yourself half stumbling to your ship with a machine gun in one hand and a flight helmet in the other. In order to speed the process of getting crews to the helicopters in these situations, gunners and crew chiefs were billeted together in the same hooch. Each hooch contained 10 to 12 people, 5 to 6 crews. Pilots shared their own accommodations. Emergency missions were usually the most dangerous because it meant friendly forces were in heavy contact and needed extraction or a re-supply of ammo. Sometimes the area would be so congested with jungle foliage or trees; the ground force would have to create a

111

landing zone with explosives. These zones were harder to get out of than into. The misconception people have is that helicopters take-off straight up. A helicopter needs to gain lift first, which means it requires a running start. There's not much thrill in seeing a wall of jungle in front of you and realize we're not going to get over the top. Lots of times the first attempt had to be aborted and we would try to exit a different direction. By then, we had usually trimmed the top of trees with the rotors. The blades were sturdy and could withstand a beating but this was not something you wanted to happen on a regular basis.

One mission had us re-supplying an infantry unit involved in heavy contact and running out of ammo. This was a one-ship mission and 626 got the call. We made a quick pick-up at the ammo dump then hustled to their location. It was pitch black and we had only a small strobe light guiding us in. We landed just outside their position and started tossing out cases of ammunition and grenades. We were in a bad spot and really had no time to socialize. In less then five minutes we were in, unloaded and out again. We were flying back to the base camp when I thought I saw something dangling from the skids about six feet directly below. Closer investigation confirmed my fear. We had snagged two claymore mines on the way out of the LZ. A claymore is the most destructive anti-personal mine in the U.S. Army arsenal. Its only function was to flat out kill you. I had two of them banging away under my seat. I clicked on the mike of my head set and passed this information up front. The

"Oh shit!" reply from the pilot made me aware he realized the danger too.

The mines were placed around the area where we landed to help secure the ground troops perimeter. I had a vision of some grunt scrambling hysterically after the detonator controls not knowing who or what had claimed them.

The pilot did not want to land with these things attached. Dragging them might set them off and we could not continue to fly with them bouncing off each other. To contribute to the excitement we had topped off with fuel earlier.

The pilot came up with a logical solution. He would reduce air speed and *I* would climb out on the skids and haul both the mines into the ship by their electrical leads. Somehow, deep inside me, I knew that would be his response. We could not take the chance of going lower than our 2000-foot altitude because our ship would make too good of a target in the moonlit sky. I would have to unhook my safety belt to accomplish this small task. I undid my belt, grabbed on to the machine gun mount and stepped down on the skid. I could feel the rotor wash of the main blades pushing on my back. The worst thing that could happen to me was getting hit by a sniper's lucky shot. No, the worst thing to happen would be to fall off the fucking Huey, survive and be taken prisoner. I eased my way lower to sit on the skid and wrapped my left arm around its vertical support. I located the two leads and gently pulled up. The adrenaline must have been pumping pretty well because they hardly weighed anything. One by one, I slid them under my seat and re-entered the ship. I gave the pilot a breathless "good to go" on the headset and we hustled over to the ordinance dump to drop off the mines.

The guys who worked ammo supply were constantly around. Four of them were playing cards when I walked into their shack. "I got a little something for you guys," and as I set them in the middle of their table, I added, "A couple of live Claymores." I could only hear the scraping of chairs dragged hastily along the wooden floor as I left.

LZ Gold

It was not uncommon for other helicopter groups to request support if they did not have enough aircraft to fulfill a mission. The "Black Widows," about 30 miles north of our base, had been hit pretty hard by a mortar attack and lost several aircraft. They requested help from the Little Bears to supply a ship to fly C & C. The mission called for ten Hueys from the Black Widows to land and deploy troops in an area known as the Hobo Woods. The landing area would be designated LZ Gold. These woods were part of a three-parcel area referred to as the Iron Triangle. The other two areas were the Boi Loi Woods and the Michelin Plantation. This was where the deadliest enemy activity was encountered.

To soften up resistance, artillery from the closest fire support base hammered the area throughout the previous night. Our command ship flew to the drop area to begin coordinating the insertion. The place was buzzing with other aircraft. A "bird dog" spotter plane was in the air directing targets for his two F-4 buddies as they dropped high explosive bombs in the woods adjacent to the LZ. I also saw a couple of prop planes flown by the ARVN Air Force taking up some air space. We were at 3000 feet, well above enemy fire. The real worry was colliding with other aircraft. I saw ten Hueys of the Black Widows start their approach into the LZ. Like us, they flew in a staggered position then lined up in a row, one behind the other, just before touching down. It was unusual for me not to be part of the landing group. This was my second round as door gunner on a C & C ship and I felt strange not being an active part of the assault. All ships were down and had begun to unload when the seventh helicopter in the group erupted into an orange fireball. Flame and smoke spewed into the sky preceding the sound waves of the explosion reaching our ship. There would be no survivors on the number seven aircraft. I saw the rotor blades of the two closest helicopters slowly stop spinning, badly damaged by the hidden bomb in the landing zone. I watched helplessly as one of the damaged Hueys started to burn while its crew scrambled to drag out an injured pilot, only to be cut down by enemy fire. The grunts had taken up position on the ground and were firing into the woods. Gunners expended thousands of rounds as the remaining ships took to the air to avoid any further losses. One ship reported a fire on board and went down on the way back to base camp, commencing a series of events that would lead to four families in the states to grieve. We left the area and headed back to base. I felt like I did nothing to help. We just sat above the whole mess and watched it happen. We could not even go in to pick up the wounded because of the extra radio equipment packed into our cargo area.

It was later discovered a 500-pound bomb had been placed in the landing zone and detonated during the insertion. It became obvious to everyone, with all the energy expended on making this zone safe; this is where we would come in. All the VC had to do was plant the bomb and leave one person to detonate it. It was a 500-pound bomb dropped by our air force. It did not explode on impact and had been reworked by the Viet Cong to be used against us.

Missions after this led to selecting multiple landing zones with one chosen for use at the last moment.

That night ground forces fought a fierce battle resulting in hundreds of VC killed when they attempted to overrun the newly established base. The next day 626 flew in a group of reporters anxious to print the story of the heroic battle and visit the site of this decisive victory. We had six on board, including two cameramen. After we landed, they scrambled over to a pile of bodies the grunts had gathered together in a large open grave. They were busy interviewing some officers and taking pictures. The burnt out remnants of two Hueys lay in rubble a hundred feet away. All that remained was white ash and a few recognizable pieces. The tail boom had separated from the main body of one ship and lay as a tombstone, only its black painted six-digit ID number revealing its identity. I stared at it, silently remembering yesterday's events. Movement behind me interrupted my homage.

One of the cameramen came over to shoot some film. He aimed his camera at the remains and started scanning slowly along the wreckage. The pressure in my body was beginning to build. He did not deserve to see this scene. He had not paid his dues to be out here. To him this was something to exploit for the cheap thrill of excitement. Something to flash on the television sets back home in the real world. War at 11:00! I was in a rage. He was desecrating this grave. I walked back to my ship to rid myself of this growing desire to destroy something. About an hour later we were in the air and on our way back to Cu-Chi. The media people were quiet and busy jotting down notes. The camera guy must have felt pretty brave because he was sitting on the door ledge with his legs hanging out shooting film of the countryside, the same camera guy who interrupted me earlier.

Without giving him any warning, I swung my machine gun around and squeezed off about a hundred rounds inches in front of his camera lens. My machine gun thundered and flames came out the barrel. I never saw anybody move so fast. He became the smallest object in the center of our helicopter. I reported to the pilot that we were receiving enemy fire and he put the ship into evasive maneuvers. I continued to fire round after round while the pilot made diving, climbing and dodging maneuvers until he felt we were out of harm's way. When I was sure the entire group of thrill-seeking journalist had made their peace with God, I let my finger slide off the trigger of my machine gun and silence returned. The heat on my face from the afternoon sun was comforting. I looked out over the countryside and saw what a beautiful country Vietnam could be.

There hadn't been any enemy fire, but I felt better the rest of the day.

The End of 626

The end of 626 came suddenly. It had proven itself in combat situations and carried the scars of self-sacrifice in its collection of patchwork plates that covered a host of bullet holes. No one cared for it more than its crew chief, Spec 5 Jerry Spurlin. Jerry and I logged a lot of flight time and over a hundred missions in it. When the ships had to be scattered throughout the base camp due to rumor of an impending mortar attack, I stayed alone with her throughout the night and we gave comfort to each other. We washed her, fed her, protected her and she returned these small services by bringing us and many others back home safely. On those rare days a mission wasn't scheduled, I spent hours sitting in the fold-down passenger seat reading a paperback book borrowed from the floating library at the base camp. I read everything from "James Bond" to "The Fountainhead." Through books I could escape the war, the army and even myself.

I felt bad not to be there at the end.

It was a milk run mission into Tan Son Nhut to pick up some nurses and return them to Cu-Chi. I was at the P.X. getting my month's supply of razor blades, soap and if I was fortunate, the latest copy of Hot Rod magazine. We had flown a mission earlier that day so the ship was still armed and ready to go. The run for the nurses came unexpectedly. The pilots decided to have a social event that night and Tan Son Nhut was where they usually recruited attendees. The mission would be logged as an administrative run. Jerry had been doing a little paint touch up job on the ship and was joined by a replacement door gunner to fill my spot. I was returning to the company area just as the reports of 626 going down began to trickle in. My mouth had a coppery taste about it. I'd gotten that same feeling the day a ship was riddled with hits and was going down over the Boi Loi woods. I heard the pilot of the doomed helicopter transmitting his position over my headset as he fought to direct the ship. A voice struggling to control fear. The tenseness and urgency in his voice still haunts me. The only good news about our ship was that no one was reported injured, but 626 was a total loss. Another Huey was dispatched to return everyone to base. Another hour passed before we got any details. I went over to the helicopter pad and waited. Luck played an undeniable role in Vietnam. I had seen a bullet pierce the chin bubble, pass through a foot pedal and stop in the pilot's boot heel. Another pilot would join the list of KIAs with one unlucky shot through his eye. I had been shot at, shot up and mortared on and managed to come through all of it with barely a scratch. Maybe the luck finally ran out for our ship. Hopefully it would not run out for us.

After 626 picked up its passengers and started its initial taxi, one of the skids caught a protruding electrical pipe causing the ship to pitch at a tight angle. The main rotor blades struck the ground then snapped back violently, cutting five feet off the tail boom. The ship rolled, ripping off the main rotor transmission. A personal loss to me was both machine guns, ground down and distorted by the unyielding surface. A violent end to violent weapons.

Jerry and I visited the site the next day to salvage whatever we could. The ship had been uprighted. With the short stubby remainder of a tail boom and no rotor assembly, it looked like a large green guppy. I felt bad for Jerry as he glanced over the mechanical corpse. He had spent as many hours maintaining the ship as he did flying in it. Six two six may have been just another Huey to most, but to Jerry and me, it was a lot more than that.

Michelin Plantation

The Michelin Plantation made up part of the Iron Triangle. Mechanized units were constantly running into tank traps or over powerful mines. Booby traps were planted throughout the area with the intent to wound rather than kill. The VC understood that by injuring someone, another person would have to see after him, eliminating another person from combat. They also knew that a helicopter would probably show up to evacuate the wounded. If he played a wait and see game, he might make a big score for the day.

I was flying in Little Bear 714 after the loss of 626. We had been ferrying replacement troops and dropping off mail most the day, all ash and trash missions. Darkness would soon fall and I was looking

125

forward to some hot chow. Flying all day meant someone handed you a can of C-rations and you ate it in the air. With no doors to block the wind, getting food into your mouth could prove to be quite an endeavor. The "Chicken Soup with Noodles" I had ended up with, was the most challenging. Being cold wasn't so bad, but most of the noodles were carried off by the turbulence of the passing air before I could get them into my mouth. I gazed at them hungrily as they dangled off the barrel of my machine gun.

Lt. Zelsman had proven to be an excellent flyer. He was the AC. I forgave him long ago for the barrel in the mud incident. The crew chief from 626, Jerry Spurlin, was sitting on the opposite side of the ship manning the other machine gun.

We heard the call about fifteen minutes from base. An APC had run over a mine in the Michelin Plantation and they needed evacuation of the seriously wounded personnel. They neglected to mention the four dead GIs. We were closest to their location so the lieutenant took the call. We were flying at our usual 2000-foot altitude, but dropped down to just above the treetops and hustled to the coordinates provided by the unfortunate crew. Flying 120 knots a few feet above the treetops never gave the enemy a chance to draw a bead on us. He could hear us coming but it was hard to distinguish our direction. If we happen to pass over him, at that speed, he could not get his weapon aimed at us in time to get off a shot. The pick up point was easy to spot. There was a column of smoke coming from the burning APC. To make things more interesting, ammo inside of it was starting to explode. The grunts tried to clear a zone for us by blowing up obstructing trees with C-4 and grenades. It would be tight getting in and even tighter getting out. They all looked to be in shock when we squeezed our way down to land. Two guys toting a body wrapped in a poncho headed for the ship. "Load only the seriously wounded first," came the order from Zelsman. "We'll pick up the dead on our last run."

I got out of the ship and passed this info to the guys. They had a dull, blank look on their face with eyes that could see but not comprehend. We got four wounded and two others on board.

With no room to spare, the lieutenant pulled pitch and swung the ship around. We got a little speed up then tried to clear the trees. No way. Not enough room. He asked me to watch the tail rotor as we backed up to get a longer run. I told him to stop when leaves started to part the closest branch. He brought on the power and we made another run. The trees kept getting closer when he pulled back on the stick to abort just as the main rotor blades started to hack away at their tops. We sat back down on the ground. "We're too heavy," he shouted over my headset, "We'll have to unload a couple." Nothing I ever said was harder than telling these guys some would have to get off. They had already been through more than most people would ever be. Daylight had started to abandon us. By now every VC in the area knew what was going on. A couple of the guys got off. I stopped one and looked into his eyes and yelled over the noise of the desperately spinning rotor blades, "We'll be back!"

This time the lieutenant didn't ask me to watch the rear; he just backed up the Huey until we could feel it shake from all the foliage it was chopping up behind us. He had a genuine 1400 horsepower Pratt and Whitney turbine engine at his control and he planned to use every last bit of it. This had to be the time. He was either going to clear the woods or park us in them. He put the nose down and made the assault. At this moment I told myself I would never refer to the pilots as bus drivers again. The rotor blades screamed in agony and I could feel the ship strain as it struggled to lift. I was ecstatic to see the skids scrape the treetops as 714 rushed to the base hospital with our precious cargo.

Twice more we made the trip out and back. The last was to pick up the dead.

By the time we got back to our own mess hall, chow had ended. Flight operations had informed them a ship would be coming in late and to hold some food for us. Jerry and I took hot water and soap to wash the blood off the inside of 714. Liver is what was for dinner that night. We both passed and headed over to the EM club. I joined some seated buddies drinking beer. Empty cans cluttered the table and some had rolled on to the floor. I had a lot of catching up to do.

Incoming

It was late in 1967 and the new model Ford Mustangs had just come out. They looked more aggressive than the previous years. I looked at my watch in the dim light and could barely make out the reflected image of the dial indicating 0400. One more day about to start meant another was over. Good to be over because this was another day done in Vietnam.

Noise. Always noise. Constant artillery fire hammered away at the enemy, relentlessly depriving them of rest. The recognizable sound of outgoing rounds backed by the never-ending beating of Huey rotor blades scurrying from mission to mission was the everyday score of the war.

Lying on my bunk in the ready room I thought about the options I would get on my new car: Big motor, four-speed transmission, mag wheels and a killer 8-track stereo. Might as well load it with options. After all, it would be my 21st birthday present to myself. November 1st seemed further away than the 26 days it preceded. All I had to do was stay alive.

The ready room was quiet. In the dim light I could make out the figures of the sleeping crew. Like me, they lay fully clothed on top of their cots. Assaults on our base camp were becoming more and more frequent. The Viet Cong figured out the strategy of harassment fire too. Nothing ever really heavy, just enough to make people nervous. Tonight I was playing the counter-mortar game. It was a simple game. One helicopter crew and ship fully armed. Toss in a forward field observer and a radio-telephone operator to complement the crew. The object was to get airborne as soon as the first mortars were reported incoming and try to search out the mortar tube flashes from the attacking force, radio in their position and have our own artillery respond. Sounds good, but usually by the time we got in the air the raid was over. Hit and run. Their war fought their way.

I tried to sleep. Just as every person has a voice that is distinctive, the sound of a mortar exploding somewhere within a base camp makes its own peculiar sound. A kind of dull thump as it hits the earth, hurling bits of hot jagged pieces of iron through the air, deadly missiles that embed in or penetrate anything in its path.

I heard the first round come in. Almost two years in country made me an expert at distinguishing outgoing from incoming. I jumped up and yelled, "Incoming!" The corners of my eyes caught the movement from the rest of the crew struggling to rise. I sprinted out the door in the direction of the pad where our ship rested. The fifty-foot dash that led me over a three-foot wide drainage ditch came to an abrupt halt as the next mortar round found a small observation helicopter across the road. The aluminum and magnesium in its structure let it burn for hours like a huge holiday sparkler. All that remained was a heap of ash and twisted metal. A sight that I had become way too familiar with. From the noise of exploding rounds and shouting voices, I was able to make out the aircraft commander's order, "Hit the bunkers!" That was an easy thing for the rest of the crew to do as they had just exited the ready room, situated six feet away from the command bunker. They were safe under a multitude of sandbags and reinforced iron plates. It was another matter for me out in the open. The last time I was caught with nowhere to go, I just buried my head in the dirt face down and listened to them fall around me. I was luckier this time. I jumped into the drain ditch I leaped over earlier. Nothing fancy, your basic three-foot deep ditch with about eight inches of water in it. Just enough to flood over the top of my boots and soak my butt. The sounds of the exploding mortars convinced me that one of those things would find its way into *my* ditch. That thought pissed me off. After all, I had less than a month left in country!

Exploding shells around me launched metal through the tin roof of the hooch I had just occupied, making a pinging sound. Deadly scrap metal passed over my head as searching rounds made their way closer.

I heard a short flutter. The fluttering sound a falling mortar makes as it passes over your head and then expends itself somewhere behind you. The longer the flutter, the farther behind you it falls. I was safe. The attack would go on, but now we could fight back. The rest of the crew knew it, as they hustled out of the bunker to check out the Huey, happy to see their wayward gunner no worse from the experience. The trace of a smile and the hint of a grin from the crew made me realize how close we had become. Knowing that death could take all of us at the same instant bound us together stronger than any known metals. No one spoke of it. A few minutes later, we were in the air.

The Village

In a country where violence is an everyday occurrence, you become a violent person. After 20 months in Vietnam I did not see the changes taking place in me. I did see it in some of my friends. We were becoming cold, aggressive and self-destructive. Too often we fought amongst ourselves over trivial matters. We even had a guy unload a clip from his M-16 at someone he had a dispute with. He did not hit him, but he definitely reinforced his viewpoint. All solutions were simple. Just blow them away. There were guys that had the look of too much combat, a cold stare and a face that no longer knew how to smile. A bizarre sense of humor, "The old guy had a rake, I told them it looked like a rifle. You should have seen him bounce!" All the talk about body count and kills extended the desire to add more numbers to individual records.

The test for me came during an assault on a village believed to be VC friendly. I cannot even recall the name of it. A Viet Cong fortified village could be our worst nightmare. The enemy would not fire until our troops were almost inside the village. At this close range, the VC could pin the U.S. forces down. It would be almost impossible for artillery or air support to help without the possibility of injuring our own troops.

Search and destroy was the mission of the day. With nine other Hueys behind us, Captain Kuhlavi and I flew the lead ship in – fast and low over the adjoining rice paddies. The LZ was a short distance from the village. Just before the paddies, a voice over my headset announced Little Bear 315 took a multitude of hits from ground fire and the gunner was seriously wounded. They had to pull out of the group and head back to base. I tried to recall who was flying 315 to put a face on the gunner. It was a guy named Stoner. I looked back to see the ship peel off from the group. They were spewing liquid from hits to the fuel cell. It was being picked up by the main rotor and swirling around the aircraft. The crew chief was returning fire not realizing that his rounds were penetrating this veil of fuel. We informed him and firing from the ship stopped. We never heard from Stoner again and no one bothered to find out later. Not knowing if someone is alive is better than knowing for sure he is dead.

That was enough of an incident to have everyone anxious and vengeful. We already suffered a loss. The ships slipped into assault position as we closed in on the village. In the rice paddies I could see about a dozen people working. They were women and kids mostly. When they spotted us approaching low and at a high rate of speed, they knew our destination was their village.

That's when they did something wrong. They started to run toward the landing zone. They could have been running for weapons or they may have just wanted to protect their meager homes from being ransacked. Our troops would probably tear everything apart looking for weapons or stores of supplies which might aid the enemy.

Flying in the lead ship, I knew that whatever I did would be repeated by the ships behind me. The order, "Stop them, Lazzarini!" came from the AC.

"Stop them," could mean one of two things. I could open fire and drop most of them. The ships behind me would follow suit. The power was in my hands to take their lives. Killing was easy. Just pull on the trigger. I could talk about it for days to come, how I blew a bunch of gooks away for taking out 315.

I laid down a long burst of rounds. The water from the paddies threw up a liquid wall as the bullets penetrated the surface. I fired directly in front of the stampeding herd of villagers bringing them to an abrupt halt. If they moved once more, they would die.

No other fire was received upon our group as we deployed the troops and exited the landing zone. I never knew what they found in that village, or if the suspicions it aided the enemy were true. I only knew that I didn't lose the ability to control my emotions and tried to retain some perspective. What I did not realize was it would be years before I would ever have deep feelings about anything again. A silent coldness and anger would replace everything. Everything.

Day-to-Day

The everyday missions made time pass quickly. Not everyone was a combat assault. The troops in the field needed food, ice, mail, ammo, replacements, even entertainment. The entertainment would sometimes be provided by a group of young women who had joined the Red Cross for that specific reason. They were mostly in their late teens or early twenties, about the same age as us. We referred to them as "Donut Dollies," because donuts were usually present. It was a tradition dating back to World War I. It was sad that a lot of us did not take them too seriously at the time. They gave up a few years of their lives to try and do something to show their support for us fighting a war in a foreign country and some of us just sort of blew them

137

off. We were becoming cynical and sarcastic. Maybe it was because they were something we could not have. They were fresh, cute and totally unobtainable. No one I knew ever had sex with any of them, so how could they be real? R & R introduced a lot of us to the wonders and joys of legalized sex in such countries as Thailand, Singapore and Taiwan. You could make arrangements with the bartender to purchase services of their in-house prostitutes. These women were our own age, monitored and taxed by the government and examined after every client. We treated these girls like we did the war; get in, get it done and party afterwards. They also acted as tour guides to show us around their country and made sure the merchants of goods or souvenirs would not overcharge us.

The Red Cross girls were trying to cheer us up with games and anecdotes. They went out to the desolate bases and shared danger and hardship same as us. Sadly, these well-meaning and wonderful women would lose a few of their own.

Only about 40 to 65 percent of the troops in country were actually involved directly with the fighting. The rest were among the thousands of men and women who supplied support. It may come to many as quite a surprise, but not everyone sent to Vietnam fired his weapon at the enemy or even saw an enemy soldier. At the height of involvement in 1969, there were over 540,000 men in Vietnam. Only about 45,000 GIs were directly involved in fighting on any given day.

I recall flying to an air force base south of Saigon to pick up a piece of equipment. It was about noon when we arrived and the air force officer we dealt with invited us to join his men for lunch. We were hauling around a picked-through case of C-rations expecting whatever was left to be a noontime meal and did not have to think twice about accepting his generous offer. Jerry and I fell in line at the EMs mess hall while the pilots followed our host over to the officers' area. The mess hall itself looked like the inside of a large airplane hanger. It was well lighted with cement floors, plenty of room and guys serving food in clean white chefs' attire. Standing in line with our M-16s hung over our shoulder and wearing faded green cotton fatigues, worn and ripped from the abuse of jumping in and out of Hueys, I became aware of a peculiar difference. The airman in front of me had a .45 holstered on his gun belt. Ammo occupied every loop of it. This was no big deal to me but every shell casing looked like it had been polished. It was then that I noticed the razor sharp crease on his heavily starched green fatigues. These guys must have had quite a laundry service because they all looked like they were ready for a parade. Shiny black boots too! I glanced down at my own footwear and admired the way little strips of dull black leather flapped in unison with every step. I was beginning to feel the way a shaggy stray pooch must feel when he accidentally strolls into a dog show. Sitting down at a table with Jerry, I asked him if these guys were fighting the same war as us. He was well aware of the differences too.

Flying back to our base camp later that afternoon, I enjoyed the feeling of the hot Asian air passing over my body. As the colors of the Vietnam countryside filled my eyes for miles and miles, I thought about those air force guys. I relaxed with the sound of the rotor blades popping over my head, raised the visor on my flight helmet and let the soothing rays of the sun flood over my face. The ship's slight vibration as it passed through the air was like a constant gentle massage that could easily lure you to sleep. Those poor air force guys. They didn't know what they were missing.

Leaving Vietnam

We were flying into the city late afternoon and I was looking over the river that runs into Saigon. Five days earlier, I received orders to return to the states for the purpose of being discharged from the U.S. Army. I was relieved from flying any more missions, but I asked my buddy Billico if I could replace him as gunner for this flight. A simple run that used up more fuel than ammo. I loved flying. The wind was blowing past my perch and I looked out over the barrel of my machine gun thinking to myself, "This is the last time I will ever do this." It was a feeling tinged with sadness. The crazy, deadly game was drawing to an end. An array of mixed emotions. Happy to be going home, sad to be leaving friends. These friends protected each other while expecting no form of payment. Pilots, crew chiefs and fellow gunners would continue to fly without me to protect them. It was as if I was running out on them. In the twenty-one months I was in Vietnam, I had become accustomed to the heat, the rain, the bugs, the sounds and the war.

No one had to tell me how much I pushed my luck. I was one of the few gunners not to be killed or wounded.

My final night turned out to be drunken gathering of officers, gunners, crew chiefs and whoever else entered my hooch. Even the enemy showed me a little respect by not dropping in mortars. We were well anesthetized anyway and I'm sure no one felt any pain. Bottles of Stoli vodka, Jim Beam bourbon, and some unnamed scotch managed to find its way over. This was the first time all forms of formality were dropped. I felt honored to call an officer by his first name instead of "sir." We were all equal, we were all one, and we were all brothers. They turned out to pay me respect, the kind you get by putting your life on the line for someone else. The kind of respect no one at any time in the future could ever take away from me. The kind of respect men who have not been to war cannot buy, steal or lie to achieve. This was a party I would never forget. I was twenty-one years and three days old.

It was interrupted only by the temporary insanity that accompanies war. I was informed that two of my friends got into an argument and were going to shoot it out on the airfield. One guy checked out a few clips of ammo for his M-16. The two of them had not been seen since they left the celebration. I felt an obligation to both of them. They were my friends. I could not leave Vietnam knowing I did not do something to stop one from killing the other. I left the party and crossed the road leading to the airfield. Only the stars punctured the black night. I could see the silhouettes of the Hueys, resting silently in their sandbag-protected enclosures. It was quiet and eerie as I walked down the rows of ships paralleling the runway. I called out their names, hoping they'd recognize my voice. I thought how ironic it would be for me to be killed by one of my friends as I searched down the field. I was anticipating the sharp sound of an M-16 being discharged, then the sharp pain as the projectile tore through my body. I would be dead. Killed, not by a friend, but by the total insanity of war in a far-off place.

A stirring in front of a bunker caught my attention. It was Jim Watson, one of the guys I was calling out to. He was sitting cross-legged up against the sandbags clutching his M-16. He recognized me. I went over to sit by him and we started to talk. The conversation centered on hate, anger and "killing that fucking bastard." I can't recall my conversation with him past those remarks. I did manage to get him to calm down and together we left the airfield to rejoin my party. I do not know if Jim would have killed anyone that night. I did know that he was afraid of something. Not of the guy he had threatened to kill but of something he may have felt hovering over him, like a clinging dark mist hidden by the black night. He had a premonition he could not shake, and it scared the hell out of him. He should have stopped flying but he continued after I left Vietnam.

It was in the only letter I received from John Bettinger, later informing me that Jim's helicopter was shot down. He had been severely injured and would be crippled for the rest of his life.

A few weeks after my departure, the Tet Offensive began.

There remained an emotional emptiness long after I returned home. I remember looking out from the window of a military transport bus after it had picked me up at Travis Air Force Base. Going down a four-lane highway for the first time in almost two years and watching the vehicles passing filled with people apparently untouched by events half a world away. "Don't they know there's a fucking war going on?" I angrily said to myself.

I left my name and phone number on the blackboard in the recreation room back at A Company. I lived close to San Francisco International Airport and hoped people would call me once they arrived. It was one of the only ways I could keep in touch with what was happening. GIs in combat are not big letter writers. The only letter I received carried the message of who was shot down and who was wounded, adding to my feeling of abandoning my buddies.

It only took a few weeks before the friends who welcomed me back home no longer had anything to do with me – except for one, Mike Kuhlman, a navy veteran of the same war. I could write another book just about our antics together. I still consider Mike to be my best friend.

I was wild, I was reckless, I was obscene. I was living on the edge for so long, I knew no other way. No one could relate to what I had done or seen. Their world was filled with petty things, fueled by illusions of who they were, disguised by what they wore. I was urged to answer stupid questions by stupid people, "Did you kill anyone?" "Did any of your friends get killed?" I simply replied, "All the people killed were my friends." That usually shut them up and I consoled myself by imagining how they would act with mortars falling and tracers seeking them out.

The war years have long since past and time has made me more lenient to the less informed. Perhaps that is why I finally decided to write this book, the story of men, mostly between the ages of 19 to 24, who ended up in one of our history's saddest and most misunderstood killing times.

The Wall holds their names, the earth holds their bodies and the survivors will never forget.

Years Gone By

In 1973, I started trying to write about the Vietnam War. The several stories I sent to publishers and magazines quickly received polite rejection notices. It seemed the rest of the world wanted to forget the war itself. I used to refer to it as the "under the rug" war.

As the years rolled by, Vietnam veterans received more attention. Perhaps it was the cloud of guilt which hung over a misled and confused generation who finally wanted to make things right. I never attended any of the functions or marched in any Veterans Day parades. To me, the U.S. media could never undo the damage it had created. Like so many Viet Vets, I just blended into the background with the knowledge of having gone through something few had imagined. I had been at war. I had gone into combat and knew how I would react under fire. I was not a hero, but not a coward either. There would never be any doubt in my mind how I would react in a life and death situation. It gave me tremendous amount of faith in myself. I know that whatever tragedy or catastrophe may strike, I can save my family and friends.

In 1985, I was working as a manager in a small restaurant in San Rafael, California. One of the customers who came in for lunch was a well-dressed and striking Asian woman. The hostess was curious as to her nationality. After discovering she was Vietnamese, the hostess informed her that the manager was a Vietnam veteran. I was summoned to her table. The woman asked where I had been stationed and what years I was there. After giving her the information, she told me she had lost two husbands in the war, both aviators. She then said something that made me invent a reason to excuse myself. I returned to my office and closed the door. Perhaps it was the flood of memories or the words she had spoken so honestly that reduced me to tears. She said, "I would like to thank you for fighting for my country."

In the 18 years I had been back from the war, this was the first time anyone had ever said that.

My Buddies

In 1969, the 25th Aviation Battalion received the "Best Aviation Unit In the Army" award from the Army Aviation Association of America. The 25th Aviation Battalion departed Vietnam on December 7, 1970 and returned to Schofield Barracks, Hawaii.

Although some of the names of people, military units, or LZs were changed, the events described in this book are real. To find out more about the Vietnam War and the 25th Aviation Battalion Little Bears, you can visit the award-winning website of Ron Leonard at http://25thaviation.org.

The following is a list of some close friends I flew with in Vietnam. We were exposed to the same danger, lived the same life-style and survived over 250 missions each. Most were never recognized for their deeds of heroism or valor at home but they served their country in the **highest traditions** of the military service:

John Bettinger	Mike King
Andy Carr	Jack Zelsman
Walter Billings	Tony Rentz
Jerry Spurlin	Tom Tull
Richard Oglesby	Bill Taylor
John Gantt	Charles Dunn
John Kulhavi	Jim Phelan
John Beam	Ben Brint
Dave Budde	Richard Muccioli
Gene Nix	Bob Masterson
Cecil McElveen	Dean Cartre
James Harris	Jan Moore

Little Bear Memorial

On Sunday August 1st, in Canton, Illinois at the entrance to the Canton Airport, a UH-1 helicopter wearing the marking of the A Company Little Bears and the 25th Infantry Division was dedicated to the memory of one of the most decorated helicopter groups of the Vietnam War.

Order Form

Please send to: Name_____

Address_____

City, State, Zip_____

_____ Soft cover copies of *Never Trust A Man In Curlers*
ISBN 1-891555-01-4 $9.95 each for a total of $_____

_____ Hard cover copies of *Highest Traditions*
ISBN 1-891555-02-2 $18.95 each for a total of $_____

California residents, please add 7.25% sales tax $_____

Shipping (air mail) $3.50 for the first book and
$1.00 for each additional book $_____

Total $_____

Send this order form with your check or money order to:

Voyager Publishing
P.O. Box 669
Larkspur, CA. 94977